A YEAR IN THE
FRENCH STYLE

INTERIORS & ENTERTAINING
BY ANTOINETTE POISSON

Editorial Director
Kate Mascaro

Editor
Helen Adedotun

Translation from the French
Pippa Hurd

Copyediting
Penelope Isaac

Design Principle
Sarah Martinon

Book Design and Typesetting
Marie-Lou Étienne

Proofreading
Kiki in Paris

Production
Élodie Conjat

Color Separation
Les Camélions

Printed in Slovenia by Florjančič

Simultaneously published in French as
Chez Antoinette Poisson ou L'Art de Vivre au fil des Saisons

English-language edition

editions.flammarion.com
@flammarioninternational

26 27 28 6 5 4

ISBN: 978-2-08-042195-1
Legal Deposit: September 2023

This work was typeset in Garamond Premier Pro
and printed on Magno Volume 150 g paper.

Flammarion is actively committed to reducing the ecological footprint of its publications.
The book you hold in your hands was printed on paper made from wood sourced from sustainably
managed forests, using vegetable-based inks, by a printer committed to environmental protection.

Send regulation (EU) 2023/988 inquiries to latelier@flammarion.fr

BY
JEAN-BAPTISTE MARTIN
& VINCENT FARELLY

A YEAR IN THE FRENCH STYLE

INTERIORS & ENTERTAINING
BY ANTOINETTE POISSON

PHOTOGRAPHS
BY RUTH RIBEAUCOURT

FLAMMARION

FOREWORD *BY* JOHN DERIAN

IMAGINE MY SURPRISE when, in the middle of a Paris trade show, I came upon a small eighteenth-century room. Its walls were covered in the most beautiful hand-painted papers, with fabrics made into cushions or just draped by themselves. Every inch of the space was perfectly adorned with imagery—including some eighteenth-century designs that were familiar to me from my own research and work. It truly was love at first sight. I couldn't keep myself away from the *Antoinette Poisson* booth; I wanted to be continually immersed in that perfectly curated world. I took everyone I knew to their stand to experience the beauty and talent of this magical team.

Of course, I ordered everything that I possibly could. I couldn't wait to share the *Antoinette Poisson* formula—which proved to be one of the most exciting and creative things I've seen in years—with my clients back in New York. *Antoinette Poisson*'s mutual passion for antique domino papers and a way of living inspired by a past century has allowed them to create a beautiful new world for us today.

Most of the recipes in this book are loosely inspired by *La Cuisinière Bourgeoise*, an eighteenth-century cookbook that we are particularly fond of—both for the richness of its dishes and for its modernity. The rather fantastical title page translates as:

THE
BOURGEOIS COOK,

FOLLOWED *BY THE* BUTLER'S PANTRY,

FOR THE USE *OF ALL* WHO INTERVENE *IN* HOUSEHOLD EXPENSES,

Containing how to recognize, dissect, and serve all kinds of meat; interesting opinions on their qualities & how to select them.

The way to make Menus for the four Seasons, & the very latest stews, an explanation of terminology, & for the use of the Kitchen and the Butler's Pantry; & an alphabetical List of necessary Utensils.

IN PARIS,
At GUILLYN, Quai des Augustins, next to the Saint-Michel bridge, at the Lys d'Or,

MDCCLXXVI.
With the Approval, & Privilege of the King.

CONTENTS

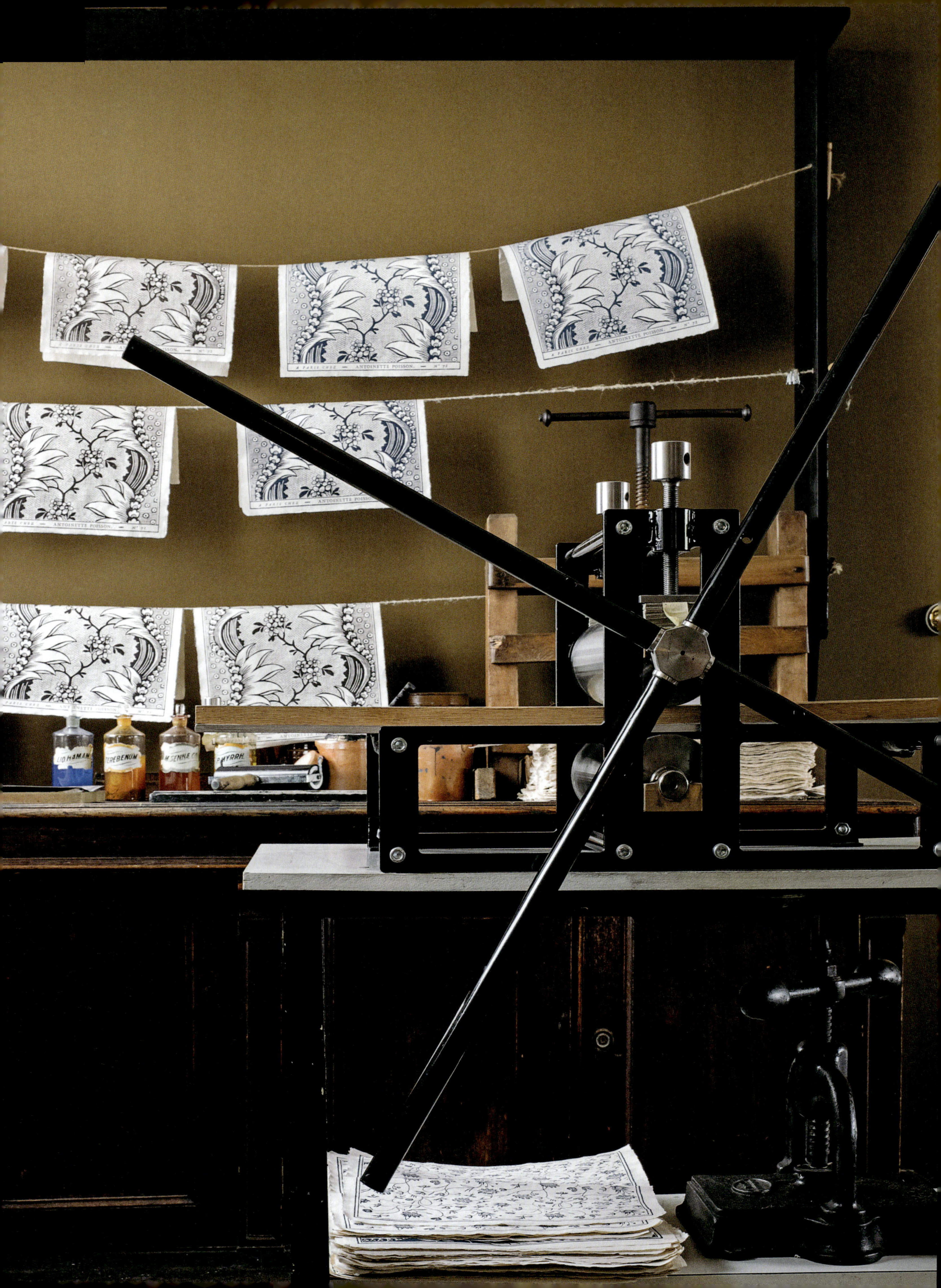
A PARIS CHEZ — ANTOINETTE POISSON. — N° 72
TEREBENUM

INTRODUCTION

The *Antoinette Poisson* workshop in Paris. The printed sheets are hung up to dry after passing through the press.

THEY SAY there is no such thing as chance, only meetings. Our path has been filled with these unexpected but significant encounters. Serendipitous (if there is such a thing), they reflect the essence of what makes up our everyday life: exchange and sharing, curiosity, creativity, passion, and friendship. The first of these meetings took place on the benches of the Institut National du Patrimoine and the Sorbonne in Paris, where our group of craftspeople came into being.

After our studies, we worked as conservators and restorers of works on paper for institutions and museums, as well as for historic residences. As time went on, we specialized in the restoration of wallpapers, working on several projects in France and abroad. The restoration of historic wallpaper interiors is a very physical job that requires the collaboration of several conservators: it involves removing dust and dirt, completely detaching the wallpaper, cleaning it in the studio, consolidating tears, lining the back of the wallpaper, rehanging it on site, repairing gaps, and retouching where necessary. We enjoyed working in this fascinating specialist area. During this time, we rediscovered many traditional techniques and a wide iconographic range of wallpapers, enabling us to expand our stylistic and historical knowledge.

On the site of a historic residence in Auvergne, we discovered fragments of *papiers dominotés*—decorative wood-block and hand-painted prints known as domino paper—beneath layers of wallpaper that had been hung successively over the centuries. In order to be able to restore them, we immersed ourselves in the history of this artisanal technique. And this led us to want to share our sense of wonder and rekindle the charm of intimate eighteenth-century interiors. For us, it seemed an obvious choice to rediscover the traditional techniques for producing domino paper and to propose it for decorative purposes. And so, after our studies and years of working in this specialist field, we undertook to revive the popular eighteenth-century tradition of *dominoterie*. As a result of this crazy challenge, our company, *À Paris chez Antoinette Poisson*, was created more than ten years ago, born out of this fascinating artistic and historical quest that we felt so passionate about. The name of our company refers to Madame de Pompadour, who was born Jeanne Antoinette Poisson. She lived from 1721 to 1764, the period when domino paper was invented. A patroness of the arts, Madame de Pompadour had a huge impact on the artists and craftsmen of her time, a period that was also influenced by the treasures recently imported from the East. After her death, the list of her effects mentions screens and printed or painted textiles known as *indiennes*.

On October 16, 1686, a decree by King Louis XIV prohibited the production, manufacture, and marketing (including import) of printed fabrics, whether cotton fabrics painted in India or counterfeit versions produced in France. This royal ban came at a time when, with the creation of the French East India Company, the fashion for *indiennes* and their techniques were competing with the woven products of France's royal manufactories. This prohibition was partly responsible for the vogue for decorative printed papers that ensued, as printing-plate engravers and fabric printers now turned their hand to this new activity. This is how domino paper, which is considered the ancestor of wallpaper, came about.

Printed mainly in black using plates, domino paper was often colored using a template (or stencil). In order to ensure the pattern continued seamlessly over the entire surface of the wall, it featured a "repeat" design that was applied to each sheet. The unprinted edges of the sheets were then trimmed away on both sides and, after applying paste to the back of each sheet, they were aligned and joined at the edges.

Due to ever-changing fashions and interiors, very few examples of these original wall decorations still exist today; they are primarily found on books from the period as, in the eighteenth century, domino paper was used by printers to cover books. As printers were not allowed to encroach on the sphere of bookbinders and gilders, who used leather, they occasionally chose to embellish their works with these patterned papers. At that time, this was called an economical cover (as opposed to a temporary binding, as such book covers are often referred to today). Printers, who could only sell books with single-sheet binding, found domino paper to be a budget-conscious and attractive substitute for case binding.

Inking the engraved plates.

A PARIS CHEZ — ANTOINETTE POISSON. — N° 72

Other kinds of objects featuring domino paper have survived: wedding chests, votive boxes made by nuns, storage caskets, and powder boxes, among others, were often covered in these fashionable patterned papers. Highly prized collector's items today, they were originally widespread and were sold by peddlers across villages and towns. Far from the well-known extravagant splendors of the eighteenth-century, domino paper transports us to a rustic, everyday world, with a touchingly old-fashioned charm.

To pursue our project, *À Paris chez Antoinette Poisson,* we needed to find a beautiful print substrate that had all the characteristics of antique paper. When we were studying materials and techniques at university, we came across Jacques Bréjoux and discovered the extraordinary work he does at his paper mill, the Moulin du Verger. Naturally, we turned to him to find the ideal paper. Since 1967, Jacques has been experimenting and working hard to become the only papermaker to produce paper pulp from old rags (essentially linen and hemp) using a hammer milling machine, which he managed to rebuild after extensive research. The Moulin du Verger produces more than just paper—it's a living material. The mill's papers are sensory objects and their "tooth" and "rattle" are beyond compare, presenting all the characteristics of seventeenth- and eighteenth-century paper.

BELOW
Paper made by Jacques Bréjoux hanging in the drying room at the Moulin du Verger.

This unique material was ideally suited for block printing the patterns that we wanted to produce. For us, the paper is as important as the pattern: they respond to each other and combine in an exchange of matter and color that satisfies the senses. Jacques Bréjoux created a paper mold for us with dimensions that corresponded to the "Couronne" format traditionally used for printing domino paper: 14⅙ × 18⅒ inches (36 × 46 cm). Once printed and trimmed on the wall, the domino paper sheets would measure 12⅗ × 16½ inches (32 × 42 cm).

We were now ready to embark on our creative adventure. We developed a color palette by studying our personal collections of antique domino papers and conducting research in various reference books. Using colored ink and a notebook, we established a "color guide," which has remained our benchmark for more than ten years.

A PARIS CHEZ — ANTOINETTE POISSON. — N° 72

A PARIS CHEZ — ANTOINETTE POISSON. — N° 72

PAGES 13–15
Printed domino paper before, after, and during hand-coloring in our Paris workshop. The pattern was inspired by an eighteenth-century original.

Working in the same way, we created a catalog of patterns, which we draw on every year to create new designs. These are either reissues of antique papers in our collection, or personal interpretations in an eighteenth-century spirit. Some traditional floral or geometric patterns have a modern feel that gives them a timeless and universal quality.

In 2013, we displayed our work for the first time on a small stand at Maison & Objet, the Paris decoration and lifestyle trade show. Young and hopeful, we had broken the bank to exhibit at this esteemed interior decoration fair. As we set up our stand, we felt very small alongside the large luxury stands around us. The contrast was striking. But fate had placed us there, amid all those prestigious decoration brands—was it perhaps one of those serendipitous meetings? At that time, the world of interior design was tending toward a return to artisanal techniques and handmade products. Unwittingly—or by chance—we arrived at just the right moment. The media immediately loved our domino paper. Renowned New York designer John Derian had noticed our work when we were setting up; he came and placed an order the minute the fair opened. This first order alone paid for our investment in the show. But it was, above all, symbolic for us; we could not have dreamed of a better "godfather" than John Derian, whose work we admire.

Our production of domino paper and of the objects we sell in many countries around the world increased exponentially. Exciting collaborations with great companies such as Confiture Parisienne, Casa Lopez, Diptyque, Gucci, and Ladurée have further enhanced our reputation.

In 2017, in response to growing demand from our customers, we developed roll wallpaper based on our block-printed domino paper patterns. We use solventless pigmented ink, which enables us to recapture the sensitivity, velvety texture, and depth of block-prints, and the subtlety of hand-painted shades. At the same time, we have begun producing coordinated fabrics, which we have printed in Mayenne on French linen woven in the Vosges département of France.

A new chapter opened for us in 2020, when Françoise Beuze—a client from the Lorient

PAGES 16–17
On one wall of a mansard bedroom in a neighboring house in Port-Louis hangs a panoramic wallpaper, "Les Monuments de Paris" (The monuments of Paris). Dating from before 1830, it was created by Joseph Dufour.

region—told us about the Breton town of Port-Louis. She extolled its charms and its varied history, intimately linked to the French East India Company, which was created in the seventeenth century. The headquarters of this commercial maritime company, tasked with bringing back treasures from the East, was located in this major fishing port, formerly called Blavet. The town was given the name of Port-Louis in 1618, under Louis XIII, and until the Revolution it would be the site of discoveries and the distribution of riches from overseas: spices, coffee, and chocolate, as well as porcelain, lacquerware, silks, and *indiennes*, which would exert a considerable influence over Western arts, in particular textiles and wallpapers. Was this yet another "chance" meeting?

Françoise produced from her bag a book called *Le Port-Louis Revisité* (Port-Louis revisited), written by the architect Gérard Dieul. On its cover, the image of a fragment of domino paper aroused our curiosity. Leafing through the book, we discovered the beauty of the buildings in Port-Louis, but also photographs of a maid's room containing a splendid set of authentic wallpapers. Through the ravages of time and the gaps that had appeared, a magnificent panoramic wallpaper revealed other, older layers. Albeit indirectly, it is thanks to this small bedroom in the attic of a pretty house once belonging to a merchant employed by the French East India Company that we decided to buy a train ticket and spend a weekend in Port-Louis.

When we arrived, Françoise told us about a historic house and its interior decoration, dating from the eighteenth century, which, she thought, perfectly suited our world. A fascinating and passionate photographer showed us around the house that he had owned for over twenty years. He had taken care to restore the original interiors and preserve its soul. It was such a pleasure for us to visit this house by the sea, which had retained its period features, having survived the centuries without being altered by less principled owners. Discovering this conservation area, this famous house, and the treasures exhibited in the museum of the French East India Company, we were enchanted and transported. Time stood still here, and we could recapture it. The era we had chosen to highlight through a forgotten skill was palpable here—so close and so alive! We returned to Paris, our heads full of projects, still intoxicated by the scent of the ocean.

Chance intervened once again. A few months later, we were lucky enough to acquire the photographer's house. We renamed it Maison Lescop, taking the name of its original owner—a merchant with the French East India Company. This authentic setting allows us to fully express ourselves, to go on celebrating the expertise of a highly creative era, sharing our passion for the eighteenth century, interior decoration, gastronomy, harmony, and friends. It's about creating a home in our image, which we would like to see filled with life. Maison Lescop has become a place of exchange and of communion around a certain vision of living in the French style.

FACING PAGE
Detail of the panoramic wallpaper, hung over many layers of older wallpaper.

Here, we have found our haven of peace, a place where we want to spend most of our time. Some members of the *À Paris chez Antoinette Poisson* team wanted to join us in this adventure, and that is how we have come to base some of our activity in Brittany.

Among this array of serendipitous meetings—and a highlight of our move to Port-Louis—we must mention François Masson. While looking for premises to set up our offices and manufacturing workshops, the sea breezes inspired us to ring the doorbell of the Tas de Sable, where François makes baroque wind instruments. François welcomed us and introduced us to his new site, which he was restoring at the time. He had acquired an old school in Port-Louis so he could bring together craftsmen and artists in need of a workshop. We have found refuge under the expansive roofs of this large building to write a new chapter in our adventure. *À Paris chez Antoinette Poisson* is also, to some extent, "À Port-Louis chez Antoinette Poisson," and we are delighted to have these two anchorages.

With love and friendship as our watermarks, this book is an opportunity to fling open the doors of Maison Lescop—a house that has captured our hearts. In a journey through the seasons, we invite you to discover the passions that drive us, the friends who accompany us, the places that move us, and the flavors that transport us, as well as our little secrets for everyday living. Let's head to Port-Louis for a journey through time in the spirit of Brittany!

—Jean-Baptiste Martin and Vincent Farelly,
founders of *À Paris chez Antoinette Poisson*

Detail of the facade of Maison Lescop, dating from the seventeenth century, with its double windows—a traditional architectural feature in Port-Louis.

ORLEA

EAU DE PARFUM
JOLI
BOIS
PARIS
CHEZ
ANTOINETTE
POISSON.
N.383
N.362
N.216

SPRING

CHOPIN
JEAN-CHRISTOPHE RUFIN
ROUGE BRÉSIL
nrf
GALLIMARD
nrf
GALLIMARD

SPRING—so long awaited—is finally on its way. Brittany's mild climate means we can enjoy the camellias and mimosas that are still blooming at the same time as irises, daffodils, and magnolia trees. The many local trackways offer a veritable firework display of blackthorn covered in blossoms and fragrant gorse.

Nature's sweet greenery, which is beginning to stir, and the promise of flowers to come are an infinite source of inspiration—the very quintessence of our work. We invite nature and its treasures indoors to embellish our homes, adorning our walls with its color palette and shapes. The entrance hall sets the mood for this ode to nature. Like a verdant theater, it opens its doors onto the different scenes in which our daily life plays out.

Spring is the season when we can finally open up the double windows that protect us from the wind and the cold. Light floods in, filling the second-floor rooms even more intensely, as if a veil has been lifted. The bathroom is transformed into an abundant, imaginary garden. The lengthening days invite us, in turn, to venture outside, and offer the eagerly anticipated opportunity to enjoy our first picnics on the beach, recalling tender memories of childhood.

A holy water stoup in the bathroom, with "Canton" wallpaper in the background.

LES AGREMENTS DE LA CAMPAGNE,
Loin du Tumulte des Villes,
On goute des plaisirs charmants
En dansant une fille agile,
Sait Captiver plus d'un Amant.

THE ENTRANCE HALL

PAGE 28
The entrance hall leads to the garden, with the kitchen on the left and the living room on the right.

PAGE 29
An Empire-period gouache engraving, *Les Agréments de la Campagne* (*The Charms of the Countryside*), hangs on the hand-painted wall.

WALKING INTO THE ENTRANCE HALL of our house is the first step on the way to giving visitors a better understanding of our world. This space immediately reflects the general atmosphere of the welcoming, wood-paneled house.

Thick planks, painted and set vertically, serve as partitions. In Port-Louis, this tradition can be seen in many houses of the same period. The simplicity of the planks highlights the beautiful finish of the Louis XV-style doors, and serves as a more rustic appetizer for the woodwork to be found in the other rooms of the house.

The entrance hall serves the two main rooms on the first floor—the living room on one side and the kitchen on the other. The far end leads to the garden through two successive glazed doors, which form a vestibule giving access to the cellar; in this space, we have created a small chapel devoted to the sea. Access to the second floor is via a simple staircase, which was probably modified in the early twentieth century. At the very top of the house, in the attic, we can see the original balustrade, most likely dating from around 1670, when the house was built.

Located between the kitchen painted in off-white and the living room where shades of pale green dominate, the entrance hall lacked character. We wanted to bring the garden and the natural world into the house, and transform the entrance hall into a centerpiece that would set the tone. It is conceived as a theater set, linking the different living areas. From the staircase and through the half-open doors, you can glimpse each of the scenes we designed to create an overall harmony. A succession of trees in the foreground lets the receding distance show through in a subtle and subdued manner, in the style of atmospheric Italian perspective views.

JOHN DERIAN

PAINTING *A* HALL MURAL

After we had sketched the overall motif in faint lines using a diluted brown paint, we had to adopt a systematic method for coloring the foliage, by applying each paint color one after the other over the entire wall. Working in this way, we were gradually immersed in a calming abundance of greenery.

As we are very fond of the colors of antique tapestries known as *verdures*, we developed five similar shades for the hall: yellow for the central sprays of leaves, followed by pale green, yellowy-green, bottle-green, and finally indigo blue for the shadows, with a few touches of dark brown to render leaves seen against the light.

We began by painting the whole entrance hall with the yellow shade, followed by the pale green leaves, and so on until we reached the brown. The trunks and branches were then accentuated using a brown tint, in order to create shadows. Using a small natural sponge, we applied a graduated shade of blue behind the branches, working from the ceiling to halfway down the wall.

The lower part of the wall, which serves as the foreground (depicting various plants and tall grasses), is merely sketched in. This incompleteness creates a kind of poetic atmosphere, as if a low mist has carpeted the ground beneath these woodland plants, leaving the treetops floating above.

In order to make this wall painting blend in perfectly with the house's original interiors, we artificially aged it by lightly sanding it with sandpaper. To soften and tie together all of the colors, the patina was finished off with a coat of tinted wax.

THE "CHAMBRE *DE L'*AMOUR"

PAGES 34–35
General view of the Chambre de l'Amour (the Room of Love), with the Louis XVI banquette seat, upholstered using the printed linen fabric known as *indienne*, and "Torrent" pattern drapes, inspired by an original eighteenth-century motif.

THIS ROOM is named for an ornamental carving on the cornice of the alcove, which evokes love and happiness with a quiver, arrows, and a cornucopia.

Divided into two differently sized spaces, this vast room consists of a large entrance boudoir and an intimate alcove overlooking the garden. To preserve the secretive nature of the alcove, we chose to hang long, floor-length drapes at its entrance. The "Torrent" pattern accentuates the two natural shades of ecru used to paint the woodwork.

The boudoir area is designed as a small living room for relaxing, meditating, and drawing, but also as a place for sharing and socializing, when it can be transformed into a game room or a tearoom. Above all, it is a space for inspiring creativity, where we like to jot down our initial ideas for new pattern collections.

In fine weather, the alcove is the ideal spot for relaxation. It's perfect, on waking, to throw the window overlooking the garden wide open, and breathe in the pure air of the sea nearby. The breeze that blows into the room gently wafts the drapes.

Thanks to the double windows typical of Port-Louis, the eighteenth-century blown-glass window in the alcove has survived throughout the ages. Some panes are marked by ancient graffiti, bearing witness to the presence of successive owners.

CLARA LUCIANI

MUSICIAN

It all started in 2019 with a Gucci shirt. Clara Luciani had to find something to wear, as she was singing on World Music Day in a performance to be broadcast on live television. In summer, it's hard to find a light, flattering garment to wear on stage. What she wanted was a chic short-sleeved shirt.

"While I was looking, I fell in love with a print that Gucci had just brought out, designed by *Antoinette Poisson*. It was lovely to see Alessandro Michele's world at Gucci, and that of *Antoinette Poisson*, as if these two universes had been fated to meet. Their approach is quite similar: two almost ancestral skills and the same desire to combine tradition and modernity. Without trying to pastiche a bygone era, they are constantly trying to reinterpret it, adding new colors and bringing it back to life. There is the same inspiration, the same fascination for the past. This seemed totally obvious to me when I made the connection between the two companies.

After the concert, we got in touch, met, and became friends. I always carry an *Antoinette Poisson* notebook, personalized with my initials, in which I sometimes write ideas for my songs. I redecorated my bedroom with the print that *Antoinette Poisson* calls 'Grenades'—the title of my most famous song. The coincidence is wonderful."

GUCCI ★ À ARLES CHEZ = G
CHEZ = GU

À ARLES CHEZ = GUCCI
★ À ARLES CHEZ = GUCCI

S CHEZ
HEZ

PEAU D'ANE
INTERIORS

STYLE TIP

CREATING *A* FLORAL BATHROOM

When we arrived in Port-Louis, we wanted to create a pattern inspired by Chinese wallpapers made in the eighteenth century in Canton. They had been imported to Europe by the East India Company, in the same way as porcelain and furniture was brought over to satisfy Europe's appetite for the exotic in domestic interiors. These wallpapers, depicting an imaginary garden, were originally hand-painted. The scenes often featured a fence in the foreground, with lots of imaginary birds, insects, flowers, and fruits. Taking inspiration from numerous eighteenth-century fragments in our archives, we created the pattern called "Canton."

For the bathroom, we chose the version of this wallpaper with a blue background, and used a lichen-colored paint on the dado and the doors with their Louis-XV moldings. This warm shade, common to certain kinds of vegetation, contrasts with the icy blue of the wallpaper. The outside of the traditional enameled claw-foot bathtub was painted in Etruscan red, adding a lively note of warmth to the colder colors used overall.

On either side of the mirror, a pair of Louis XV-style chased and gilded bronze sconces was converted to electric for bathroom use. The papier-mâché lampshades were covered using the same wallpaper.

PEAU D'ANE
HUILE DE SAVON
À LA FLEUR D'ORANGER DE BERKANE

PORTRAIT

FRANÇOIS MASSON

L U T H I E R

In his workshop near the church in Port-Louis, François Masson makes baroque wind instruments, copying mainly eighteenth-century models. With passion and expertise, he restores and creates instruments for well-known musicians. He is one of the last artisans in the world to specialize in this rare trade. He studied at Newark and Sherwood College near Nottingham in England, and has become an expert in the manufacture of these historical instruments.

After moving to Port-Louis, we began looking for a workspace, as we intended to spend more time there. Thanks to another chance encounter, François suggested that we set up our workshop in his building. Full of generosity and dynamism, François is an altruistic creative devoted to the art world. A musician himself, as well as an occasional handyman and perfectionist in all he does, he extended a warm and attentive welcome to us in his new workshop space, created with his partner Amélie.

The workspace is a former school that has been turned into a place of creativity, exchange, production, and distribution, open to craftworkers and artists. Its name, Tas de Sable, was inspired by a slang expression, "Rendez-vous au tas de sable" ("meet at the pile of sand"), used by jazz musicians to mean that everyone can improvise before returning, on an agreed signal, to the main musical theme. This is how our collaboration began, under the auspices of wonderful harmonies. And it's here that we are now writing the new musical score for *Antoinette Poisson*.

GATHERING FENNEL FLOWER BOUQUETS

OUR INNER CHILDREN have not forgotten the joy of creating bouquets of wildflowers. The simple pleasure that this activity still gives us—and the desire to share it—continues today.

Late spring is a good time to pick flowers along the roadsides, where one can find many plants of the Apiaceae family, known as umbellifers. We eagerly await the arrival of wild fennel and the glow of its yellow umbels. It's a plant we love to cook with, whether making use of its swollen bulb, its flowers, or its leaves. Fennel's aniseed flavor is the perfect partner for fish dishes.

When at last the fine weather arrives, fennel's long stems, which can grow up to eight feet (2.5 m) long, make bouquets that will add freshness and delicacy to the kitchen table.

The prospect of these fragrant feasts encourages us to explore the countryside along trackways and flower-filled meadows. The pleasures are numerous: discovering landscapes, picking and creating bouquets to decorate the house, and salivating at the thought of cooking these little treasures foraged from the natural world.

HUITRES
HUITRES
COQUILLAGES

PAGES 54–55
Parcs de Navihan is an oyster farm located near the Pont Lorois near Belz, at the mouth of the Etel River. It's a wonderful local source of oysters and shellfish. The oyster beds lie just outside the store.

FACING PAGE
The spider crab is prized for its tender, succulent flesh. It is also delicate and does not remain fresh if kept out of water for over 24 hours before being cooked, unlike its hardier cousin, the brown crab.

PICNIC *ON THE* BEACH

As spring arrives, the days get longer, so it's time to enjoy sociable evenings with friends. The small folding garden table, its wood bleached by the rain, is set up on the beach for the party. The menu includes seafood, salted butter, farmhouse bread, and a good white wine—the epitome of a Breton meal by the seaside. These picnics always seem like a little expedition; we arrive on foot, carrying all this equipment, but once we reach the small hidden cove, we quickly forget all the effort involved.

On a table runner made from an old canvas mattress cover, we have laid out our collection of plates. The red seafood looks wonderful against the bluish gray of the decoration.

The plates resulted from our collaboration with two ceramicists known as TopTop, who we met in our Paris courtyard, and who have since moved to Nantes. The idea was to create a bowl-shaped vessel that we particularly love because it can be used for anything. Molded in raw clay, the form is printed by hand using stamps and slip. Color can also be applied using a brush or stencil. We wanted to reproduce the technique of printing and coloring domino papers but on ceramics. The result is very beautiful, and each piece is unique, complete with the kind of small imperfections we adore.

A typical postcard scene in Brittany. The house with the blue shutters was built on the rocky islet of Nichtarguer, at the mouth of the Etel River. Also known as the Oyster House, it was once the home of an oyster farmer and his family. Travelers come from all over to stand on the quayside and watch the magnificent sunsets in this little corner of land with its legendary history.

MENU
Herb Soup
Skate Wing with Anchovy & Caper Butter
Almond Ice Cream

Herb Soup

SERVES 4
PREPARATION TIME: 10 minutes
COOKING TIME: 15 minutes (+ 1 hour if making homemade chicken stock)

If you are making homemade chicken stock, place the chicken carcass, bouquet garni, and water in a saucepot and season with salt and pepper. Bring to a boil and let simmer for 1 hour. Strain, return to the pot, and keep warm.

If you are using bouillon powder or cubes, combine the amount indicated on the packaging in a saucepot with 4 cups (1 liter) water. Bring to a boil and stir to dissolve. Keep warm.

Meanwhile, to prepare the soup, wash all the vegetables and herbs. Scrub the parsnip and carrot, and peel them if they are not organic.

Cut the parsnip, carrot, and celery lengthwise into thin slices. Place in the stock, bring to a simmer, and cook for 10 minutes, until tender-crisp.

Add the spinach, lettuce, and sorrel and cook for an additional 5 minutes. Season with salt and white pepper.

Divide the vegetables and herbs between four soup plates and add a ladleful of broth to each. Garnish with the chervil and serve.

INGREDIENTS

Homemade chicken stock:
Roast chicken carcass
Bouquet garni (rosemary, thyme, bay leaf, sage, etc.)
6 cups (1.5 liters) water
Salt and pepper
or
High-quality chicken bouillon powder or cubes (as needed)
4 cups (1 liter) water

Herb soup:
1 parsnip
1 carrot
1 stalk celery
7 oz. (200 g) baby spinach
8 small lettuce leaves
4 sorrel leaves
A few sprigs chervil, for garnish
Salt and white pepper

Skate Wing with Anchovy & Caper Butter

SERVES 4
PREPARATION TIME: 10 minutes
COOKING TIME: 15 minutes

INGREDIENTS

1 × 1¾-lb. (800-g) or
2 × 14-oz. (400-g) skate wing(s)
2 tbsp wine vinegar
1 onion, peeled and quartered
1 bay leaf
1 stick + 2 tbsp (5¼ oz./150 g) unsalted butter
6 anchovy fillets in oil, chopped
2 tbsp (1 oz./30 g) capers in brine
Parsley, chopped
Salt and pepper

To serve:
Steamed potatoes

Rinse the skate wing(s) under cold water.

Fill a large pot with salted water and add the vinegar, onion, and bay leaf. Bring to a boil.

Add the skate wing(s), reduce the heat, and let simmer gently for 15 minutes.

Meanwhile, melt the butter in a saucepan. Add the anchovies and capers, then remove from the heat.

Carefully drain the skate wing(s) and place whole on a serving plate. Drizzle with the melted caper-anchovy butter, sprinkle with parsley, and season to taste with salt and pepper.

Serve immediately, with the steamed potatoes.

Almond Ice Cream

SERVES 4
PREPARATION TIME: 10 minutes
COOKING TIME: 15 minutes
CHILLING TIME: 6 to 12 hours
FREEZING TIME: At least 4 hours

INGREDIENTS

1½ cups (350 ml) whole milk
2 tbsp (30 ml) heavy cream
1 heaped tablespoon (25 g) honey
4½ oz. (130 g) almond paste
3 egg yolks
Candied orange slices for serving (optional)

Pour the milk and cream into a large saucepan and add the honey. Cut the almond paste into small pieces and add to the saucepan. Warm over medium heat, whisking to dissolve the almond paste.

In a large bowl, whisk the egg yolks. Whisking vigorously, pour in the hot milk mixture all at once.

Return the mixture to the saucepan. Stirring continuously with a spatula, cook over low heat until thickened.

Set the saucepan containing the thickened mixture over a bowl filled with ice water and stir the mixture occasionally to cool it quickly. Transfer to a container and place in the refrigerator for at least 6 hours (ideally 12) to allow the flavors to develop.

If you have an ice-cream maker, churn the chilled mixture according to the manufacturer's instructions. Transfer to a freezer-safe container, or use a mold if you'd like to give the ice cream a shape. Freeze for at least 4 hours before serving.

If you do not have an ice-cream maker, pour the chilled mixture into a larger, freezer-safe container and place in the freezer. Every hour, remove and mix vigorously using a fork, to prevent ice crystals from forming. Repeat until the ice cream has set.

To serve, run the mold or container quickly under warm water and turn the ice cream out onto a serving plate. Decorate with candied orange slices if you wish.

A PARIS CHE
ANTOINETTE POISSON.

ANTOINETTE POISSON.
N°6

TOURMI Nº 2

SUMMER

It's vacation time, the season of sun-drenched days on the Port-Louis peninsula in Brittany. We spend most of the time outdoors, living life to the full.

The local market is renowned for the quality of its produce, and on the day of our visit it is well stocked and bustling with regular customers. Back home, our arms laden with food, we start the big job of unpacking our provisions on the kitchen farmhouse table: vegetables, fish, shellfish (it's high season), as well as meats and cold cuts, cheeses, and artisan breads. The scene is worthy of a Flemish Old Master painting and will set the tone for our weekend spent creating menus; the invitations are ready to be sent out.

Whether planned or impromptu, large summer parties begin outdoors, in the open air. We carry our feast outside in the wicker baskets we used in the morning at the market, and which we'll use to take everything back into the house after the festivities. Pleasure boating offers a way to escape out to the open sea or to take a trip to nearby Île-de-Groix. And when they're at anchor, these sailboats provide the ideal spot for a refreshing lunch. In the evenings, we make last-minute plans to go swimming with friends, enveloped by the warm light of the setting sun, which—until twilight—illuminates the comings and goings of sailboats returning to and leaving Lorient harbor.

In summer, the garden regains its former glory and becomes a veritable workshop for home improvements and experimentation, as we set out two trestles, some planks, and tools, to begin carpentry work for the house. We also make indigo dye using a technique that requires space and a gentle kind of heat that will protect the dyeing solution. We set up the vat in the shade of an oak tree, with piles of linen alongside. After being immersed in the dye, they waft delicately on the washing lines. These intensely blue fabrics will be used to make tablecloths and napkins for future events.

Entertaining guests, being invited in turn, sailing, and experimenting—that's our life in the summer season! This region certainly inspires such a way of living: we're becoming immersed in the maritime world of Port-Louis, and in its history, which is inextricably linked with the importation of new techniques and objects. This is where the French East India Company, created by Louis XIV in 1664, transported the treasures of Asia, revolutionizing the arts and lifestyle of old Europe. Porcelain, fabrics, spices, patterns, colors, materials, and know-how from the East have transformed European culture. From 1666 onward, Port-Louis was the gateway for these fascinating imports which we now consider essential.

Details of Chinese porcelain imported by the French East India Company. Here, the pieces are combined with delicate eighteenth-century Provençal textiles.

AFE JULES

THE KITCHEN

THE KITCHEN is without doubt the room in Maison Lescop that has required the most attention. It's an essential room, a place of sharing and socializing.

The layout of the house is very simple: on either side of the central staircase each room provides a dual aspect onto both street and garden. The front windows once formed a perfectly symmetrical facade. In the 1950s, the room to the left of the staircase was converted into a garage, and the wood paneling was partly removed. Later, in the 1990s, this garage was divided up into four smaller spaces (bathroom, small kitchen, darkroom, and boiler room). We felt it was both obvious and necessary to reinstate this room's original scale. Rebuilding the facade and recreating a new window gave us the opportunity to restore the seventeenth-century symmetry. We knocked down the modern partitions forming these various small spaces, thus making available some 290 square feet (27 m^2) in which we could create the kitchen.

We wanted to design a living space that would fit in perfectly with the rest of the house and give the impression that it had always been there. Our aim was to reproduce the feel of a genuine, old-fashioned kitchen, with woodwork in the style of the epoch. For that, we opted for rows of low units. Thanks to Romain Chauveau and Supercraft, his interior design studio, as well as Golfe Agencement, a local carpentry company, all the cupboards feature moldings whose pattern was inspired by a cabinet fitted into

Antique copper and tin-plated iron molds are displayed on the painted wooden shelves, with lids and a mixing bowl hanging below.

the paneling of the living room. Like eighteenth-century cabinets, each row of units has rounded corners. The edges of the oak worktops are embellished with *bec-de-corbin* or "billhead" molding, again in the eighteenth-century style. Simple wooden shelves, painted to match the colors of the kitchen, are used to display copper pans and molds on one side, and plates, glasses, and cutlery on the other. Above the stove, a wooden extractor hood casing provides a visual echo of the fireplace in the living room.

As for the overall paint color, we worked with the brand Ressource to develop a single shade of off-white that beautifully enhances the copper utensils.

In the center of the kitchen, which we designed as a dining space, a very large vintage pantry table takes pride of place. It immediately imposes its presence, while also making it clear that this is a place of true hospitality.

Breton blue lobster is distinguished by its midnight blue color and the yellow marks on its head. Its flesh is extremely delicate.

FACING PAGE
Food simmering gently over the burners on the range. The extractor-hood casing was made to measure by a local carpentry company.

PAGES 90–91
The huge vintage table, with its incredible patina, is nearly ten feet (3 m) long and forms the centerpiece of this kitchen. It's an invitation to share and socialize.

STYLE TIP

STORING DISHES

In addition to providing storage, kitchen shelves can also be used to display serving dishes, glassware, and copperware. To store plates or dishes, an old system used in pantries consists of two regularly spaced rows of round wooden rods or dowels set vertically between two shelves. The spacing depends on the diameter of the plates to be displayed.

Before we attached the shelves together, we drilled holes for the rods ⅜ in. (1 cm) deep to secure the rods between the upper and lower shelves. The ends of the rods were glued, then placed in the holes in the shelves before assembling the shelf unit. It was then painted the same color as the walls. This system allows the plates and dishes to be stored safely, protected from possible damage, while also displaying them attractively. We fixed our unit above the second kitchen sink, which is used exclusively for tableware.

EAU
NON POTABLE

EAU
NON POTABLE

1000 Gr

The garden of the house is enclosed by high walls and conjures up the charm of a *jardin de curé*. South-facing, it can be enjoyed all year round. When summer comes, we like to take out an oil lamp to illuminate the table and hang a string of lights in the euonymus and camellia bushes.

A "COMPAGNIE *DES* INDES" TABLE

Summer is the season for colors that are both bold and refreshing. There's nothing better than an indigo-dyed hemp or linen tablecloth to dress up a table. The technique for creating this distinctive shade of blue was imported to Europe from the seventeenth century onward by the various East India Companies; it perfectly matches the Chinese porcelain being imported at that time.

Blue and white decorative designs are commonly found on Chinese porcelain made for export during the seventeenth and eighteenth centuries. The intense blue is the result of firing cobalt oxide at 2552°F (1400°C). Colored porcelain pieces (fired at high temperatures of 2462°F [1350°C]) featuring a shade of green often derived from copper oxide, as well as red, yellow, blue, and purple enamels, complement the palette of blues, adding energy and flamboyance. They can be used in non-matching combinations, with table napkins made from scraps of vintage floral textiles and with artisanal glassware such as pieces by La Soufflerie. The latter is a Parisian company that produces stemmed glasses, whose shapes are inspired by vintage glassware and harmonize perfectly with all styles and eras.

On the table, a few cornflowers—very popular in the eighteenth century—delicately enhance this travel-inspired setting.

French East India Company
Chinese porcelain plates are combined
with delicate napkins made from
eighteenth-century Provençal fabric
on an indigo-dyed hemp tablecloth.
On a summer's day in the living room,
this elegant, refined table setting
conjures dreams of travel.

FRANÇOISE BEUZE

INDIGO DYER

In January 2020, Françoise—a loyal customer who has become a friend—walked into our store and passionately described the town of Port-Louis to us, with its museum of the French East India Company, and a merchant's house that had retained its original interiors. Aware of the importance of preserving our architectural heritage, Françoise hated the idea that this house might fall into the hands of inexperienced buyers who would not know how to respect the spirit of the building. She thought it was perfect for us and so launched us on our adventure. And she was absolutely right! This house was made for us. We adore Françoise: she has always been interested in beautiful craftsmanship and antiques, as well as making discoveries overseas, in New Caledonia and Guyana where she has lived. She is an artistic, inquisitive, generous soul, who travels extensively, in particular to Japan—a great source of inspiration for her work using indigo, and for the traditional Japanese *boro* textiles that she collects.

Françoise loves nature and walks in the woods. She also has her mushroom "spots," and when we visit her, she very generously shares them with us. Ceps, girolles, and chanterelles are wonderful treasures that can be foraged in the undergrowth, sometimes until early summer, weather permitting, and then again in fall.

STYLE TIP

CREATING *A* HIDDEN DOORWAY

THE RENOVATION WORK taking place in the kitchen gave us the opportunity to create a bathroom on the ground floor. We set aside about twenty-one square feet (2 m^2) of the kitchen to create this bathroom with an entrance near the front door.

To avoid disrupting the harmony of the entrance hall and the symmetry of the Louis XV doors, a new opening was cut into the eighteenth-century wooden boards that make up the walls. These boards have an incredible surface finish. Chisel marks in the wood become visible in low-angled light, bearing witness to the craftsman's work and conveying a beautiful sense of artistry.

Our carpenter cut a hole in the wall where the future doorway was to go. He then repositioned the boards, arranged exactly as they were, and fixed them to a simple door whose frame faces inward, into the bathroom.

The secret door almost completely disappears, camouflaged by a wall painting of woodland plants.

JOHN DERIAN

DECOUPAGE ARTIST

Since 1989, John Derian has been using decoupages of engravings to create furniture and glass-topped objects in his New York studio. His work and his various ceramic collaborations with Astier de Villatte are on display in his Manhattan emporiums, surrounded by the antiques he sources mainly from France.

In the early days of *Antoinette Poisson*, John Derian was, in a way, our guiding lucky star. When we launched the *À Paris chez Antoinette Poisson* brand at the Parisian decoration and lifestyle trade show Maison & Objet in January 2013, John discovered us by chance. When he placed his first order at the fair, it was important for two reasons: it gave us a presence in New York and John's order alone covered our investment to participate at the show.

Ever since our fortuitious meeting in Paris, John has continued to stock a selection of *Antoinette Poisson* objects in his charming, Aladdin's cave of a shop in New York. This temple of good taste has opened many doors for us that, at the time, we could scarcely dream of.

Der grosse Lori.
Der gelbe Sittich

CUCURBITA

Fig. 2.
Fig. 2.
Fig. 1.

CREATING *A* *SEA* CHAPEL

WE ALL HAVE MANY OBJECTS that we've accumulated in boxes or on shelves, sometimes collecting dust without being appreciated. When we were moving in and unpacking our boxes, we began putting to one side photos and souvenirs that didn't necessarily find a natural place in the house. While considering how to decorate a small, overlooked space between the entrance hall and the garden, we came upon the idea of creating a setting for these objects. There was something quite charming about this in-between space that hinted at its potential.

The door with its rounded top has a small boat's porthole in the center. We imagined creating a little devotional chapel filled with souvenirs—objects that spoke of navigation, travel, and prayer. In order to showcase these objects, we used a striking color on the walls. The matte finish adds a lot of depth. The blue-gray color that we developed with Ressource is reminiscent of raging waves on the high seas—a perfect shade for our theme.

The art of this space is about collecting objects and charming souvenirs that we wanted to preserve by giving them a second life on one single, colorful wall. It guarantees a decorative impact and it's very easy to achieve.

Our collection of objects is showcased wonderfully against this wall painted blue-gray to evoke the sea. Italian silver ex-votos and family photos are hung side by side.

F
GER
270

SETTING SAIL

LORIENT'S MARITIME IDENTITY is linked to its geographical position but also to its history.

In 1666, the newly founded French East India Company, which had been created in 1664 by Jean-Baptiste Colbert, was given land by Louis XIV to set up its facilities in the hamlet of Le Faouédic. From 1688 onward, the royal navy located itself in these shipyards to build boats. Legend says that the first ship to leave the yard, *Le Soleil d'Orient*, gave its name to the future town of Lorient. Many ships were built by the Arsenal of Lorient over the following centuries (including France's first battleships). As the fishing industry began to develop in the 1920s, the town flourished. During World War II, the occupying forces chose Lorient as the location for the largest submarine base of the time, which would lead to the town's near total destruction during the Liberation.

Today, sailors from all over the world meet in the bay in July every year. It has more than ten ports and is located in the south of the Morbihan département, between two coastal inlets: the Etel to the east and La Laïta to the west. It's a wonderful playground for nautical leisure activities.

Cousins Paskal and Éric Morvan are two enthusiasts who both have a sailboat moored at Port-Louis. One August evening, they shared a magical crossing to Île-de-Groix with us, aboard Éric's Nordic Folkboat. To thank them, we had prepared a basket of oysters and homemade smoked salmon that we enjoyed on board. Served on aluminum tableware, this picnic at anchor off the red sand coast of Île-de-Groix remains a wonderful memory of treasured friendship.

On that delightful evening, the hours flew by, and we had to get back to the mainland. We had certainly taken our time, but it turned out to be for the best: we spent the return trip gazing at a marvelous sunset and admiring a sea of *glaz*. This Breton word, which has no direct translation in English, refers to an indefinable color somewhere between green, blue, and gray—a color that changes with the tides and the sun. It's a shade that you can see and feel only by appreciating the poetry of the moment.

6CR

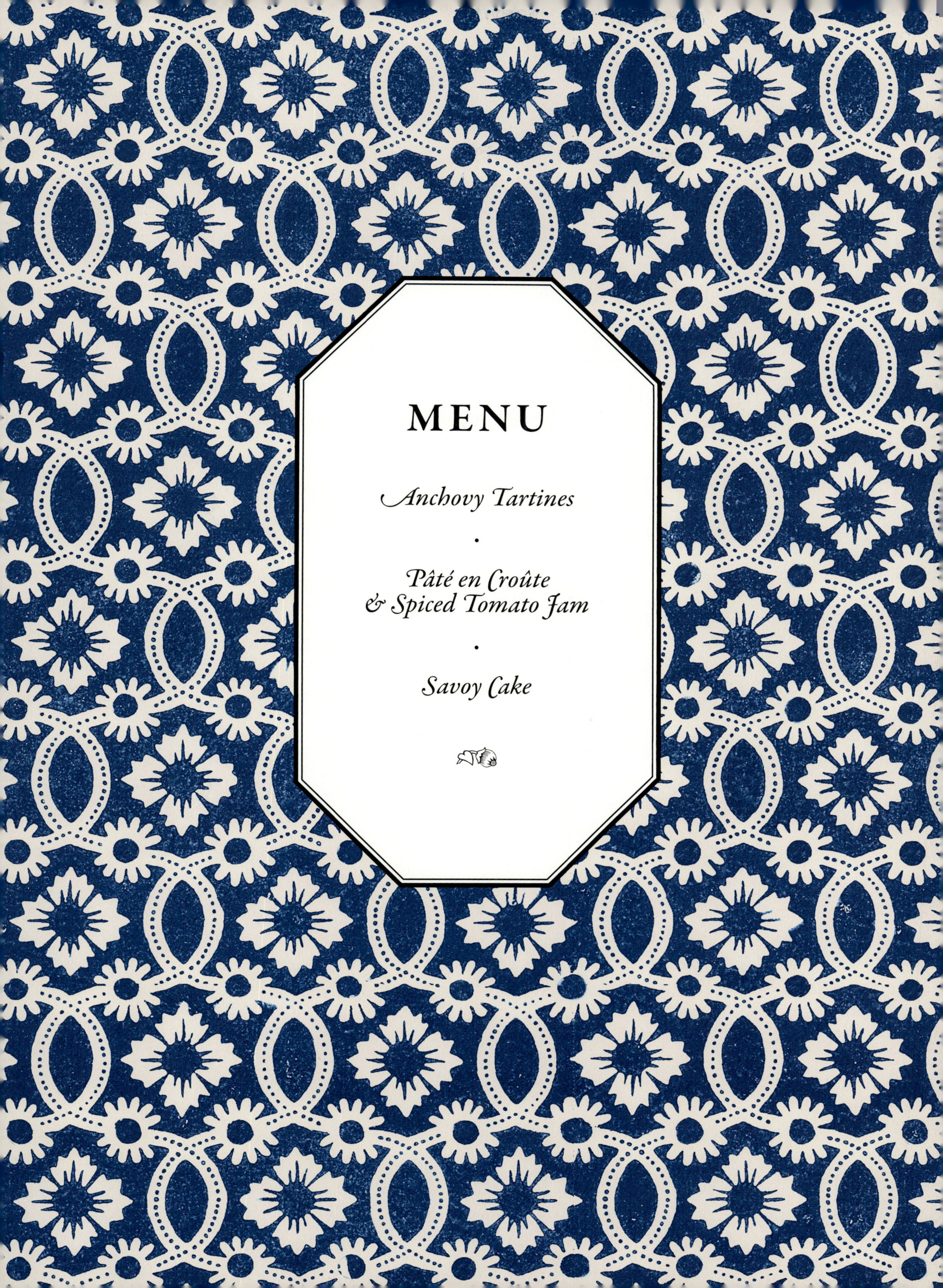
MENU
Anchovy Tartines
Pâté en Croûte
& Spiced Tomato Jam
Savoy Cake

Anchovy Tartines

SERVES 4
PREPARATION TIME: 10 minutes
COOKING TIME: 5 minutes

INGREDIENTS

A few sprigs flat-leaf parsley
1 shallot
A few scallions
4 slices country bread
Lightly salted butter
12 to 16 oil-packed anchovy fillets
Freshly ground pepper

Preheat the broiler.

Finely chop the parsley and shallot, and thinly slice the scallions.

Butter the bread slices on one side and place butter-side-up on a baking sheet. Toast under the broiler until deeply browned.

Remove the toasted bread from the oven and scatter with the parsley, shallot, and scallions. Arrange the anchovies diagonally over the top. Season with pepper to taste.

Paté en Croûte & Spiced Tomato Jam

SERVES 6
PREPARATION TIME: 2 hours
COOKING TIME: 1 hour
CHILLING TIME: 2 nights
(overnight for raw pastry and overnight for completed pie) + 30 minutes

EQUIPMENT

8-in. (20-cm) round pâté mold, 4 in. (10 cm) high (alternatively, use a flan mold); about 5 jam jars, sterilized

INGREDIENTS

Pastry (make 2 days ahead):
2 cups (9 oz./250 g) all-purpose flour
¾ cup (4 oz./115 g) cornstarch
3½ oz. (100 g) duck fat, well chilled
1 stick + 1 tsp (4 oz./120 g) salted butter, well chilled and diced
Scant ½ tsp (2 g) sugar
1 egg
¼ cup (60 ml) water
1 tsp (5 ml) white wine vinegar

Filling (make 1 day ahead):
3½ oz. (100 g) chicken breast
2 tsp (10 g) crème fraîche (preferably raw)
1 lb. (450 g) pork belly
5¼ oz. (150 g) duck foie gras (raw or partially cooked [*mi-cuit*])
4 tbsp (60 ml) cognac
1 egg yolk
8 sheets gelatin
2 cups (500 ml) water
2 chicken bouillon cubes
Salt and freshly ground pepper

Spiced tomato jam (make 1 day ahead):
2¼ lb. (1 kg) tomatoes
2¼ cups (1 lb./500 g) packed brown sugar
2 tsp salt
4 tsp Kari Gosse curry powder (or use 1 tsp each of ground ginger, turmeric, cinnamon, and chili powder)

Prepare the pastry two days before serving the pâté en croute. Combine the flour and cornstarch and make a well in the center. Break the duck fat into pieces and add with the butter and sugar. Work in using your fingertips, until the mixture has a coarse, crumbly texture. Make another well in the center and add the egg, water, and vinegar. Gradually draw the flour into the well until all the liquid is absorbed. Knead briefly until well combined, shape into a ball, and cover with plastic wrap. Chill overnight.

The next day, prepare the filling. Preheat the oven to 380°F (195°C/Gas Mark 5). Chop the chicken breast and place in a food processor with the crème fraîche. Season with salt and pepper and process until smooth. Finely chop the pork belly and place it in a bowl with the cognac. Season, stir to combine, and set aside. Cut the foie gras into thick slices.

Roll the pastry to a thickness of ⅛ inch (4 mm). Generously grease the pâté mold with butter and line it with the pastry. Trim off the excess, leaving a ½-inch (1-cm) border above the rim. Reserve the remaining pastry for the top.

Add the filling in successive layers. Start with half the pork-belly-cognac mixture, followed by half the chicken mixture. Top with the foie gras slices, then add the remaining pork-belly and chicken mixtures in layers. Whisk the egg yolk with a little water to make an egg wash. Cover the pâté filling with the remaining pastry, using a little egg wash to seal the edges together.

Make a small chimney in the center of the pastry lid to allow steam to escape. Score a design in the surface using the tip of a knife. Brush the top with egg wash and bake for 50 minutes to 1 hour, until deeply golden.

Meanwhile, soak the gelatin sheets in a bowl of cold water to soften. Heat the 2 cups (500 ml) water in a saucepan and stir in the bouillon cubes. Squeeze excess water from the gelatin and stir it into the hot liquid until dissolved. Keep warm.

Remove the pâté en croute from the oven and let rest for 30 minutes. Pour the broth into the chimney in three equal quantities. Chill overnight.

For the spiced tomato jam, inspired by François Roy, quarter the tomatoes and place in a large bowl. Add the brown sugar and salt and stir gently to coat. Cover and chill overnight.

The next day, transfer the tomatoes to a large saucepan and add the spices. Cook over low heat, stirring often, until the liquid has evaporated and the mixture is thick. Pour into the sterilized jars and seal tightly.

Briefly warm the pâté en croute mold over a gas burner to make it easier to remove the pâté. Serve with the spiced tomato jam.

Savoy Cake

SERVES 6
PREPARATION TIME: 20 minutes
COOKING TIME: 40 minutes
RESTING TIME: 1 hour after baking

EQUIPMENT

9½-in. (24-cm) Savoy cake pan
or Bundt pan (preferably copper)

INGREDIENTS

Sponge:
Butter and sugar to line the pan
6 eggs
¾ cup (5 oz./150 g) sugar
Zest of 1 lime
1 tbsp orange blossom water
¾ cup + 2 tbsp (3½ oz./100 g)
all-purpose flour

Glaze:
1 generous cup (5¼ oz./150 g)
confectioners' sugar
1 egg white
Juice of ½ lemon

To serve:
Strawberries and carrot flowers

To prepare the sponge, preheat the oven to 350°F (180°C/Gas Mark 4). Grease the cake pan with butter and coat with sugar.

Separate the egg yolks and whites into two different large bowls.

In the first bowl, to the egg yolks add the sugar, lime zest, and orange blossom water, and whisk until pale and thick. Sift in the flour and fold in until just combined.

In the second bowl, whisk the egg whites until they hold firm peaks. Gently fold them into the batter.

Pour the batter into the prepared pan and bake for 35 to 40 minutes, until the cake is golden, and a knife inserted into the center comes out clean.

Let the cake cool in the pan, then turn it out onto a serving plate.

To prepare the glaze, stir all the ingredients together using a wooden spoon until smooth and white.

Pour the glaze over the cake and decorate with strawberries and carrot flowers. Let the glaze set before serving.

A PARIS

— MUSEE DE MEZIERES (CH) —

HEZ — ANTOINETTE POI

44

EAU DE PARFUM
TISON
A PARIS
— CHEZ —
ANTOINETTE
POISSON.

FALL
A PARIS CHEZ — ANTOINETTE POISSON. — N°24

EANS CHEZ

THE HIGH TIDES of the equinox signal the arrival of fall, and the shortening days mean we spend more and more time in the living room. The damper weather brings the emergence of the first fungi of the season, encouraging us to head out on mushroom-gathering expeditions. Then, after long walks in the woods, we enjoy watching the flames dancing in the fireplace once more. It's a chance to huddle around the fire and share our woodland harvests. Our baskets overflow with girolles, chanterelles, porcini, boletus, and chestnut mushrooms.

Rainy weekends provide a perfect opportunity to visit flea markets, where we always hope to unearth some charming objects that might find a place in our house. We have always endeavored to resist the standardization of everyday life, which is so prevalent nowadays, and overconsumption is a concern that worries us. The times we are living in make us dream of another era—like a kind of sweet nostalgia that offers us new inspiration. Thanks to the values our parents instilled in us, we have learned to consume little, and to reuse and repair rather than to throw away. Objects from the past, to which we attribute an imagined "life," have an extra-special quality that we find seductive.

Visits to some private dealers take us further afield, even as far as the département of Finistère. We love discovering Brittany's parish enclosures, with their majestic wayside depictions of the Crucifixion, known as *calvaires* (calvaries), as well as hamlets whose delightful chapels house inspiring painted-wood baroque altarpieces. Back in Port-Louis, we have fun deciding on the ideal spot to display the treasures we've discovered.

The soft autumnal light that lasts until Christmas brings out the beauty of this little corner of Brittany, tucked between land and sea. While the ocean gradually turns gray and the waves are crested with white foam, the oaks and chestnut trees in the forest burst into dazzling color. Yellows, ochers, reds, and purples create a dazzling spectacle in the gently fading light. These warm colors provide us with inspiration for decorating the house, and we decided to feature them in one of our bedrooms.

An exceptional account book from a mill that was active in the eighteenth-century, covered in a floral domino paper from A Paris chez les Associés, is placed on a silver platter. It is topped by a charming almanac cloaked in a domino paper from A Orléans chez Letourmy.

JOHN DERIAN

ANTOINETTE POISSON.

THE LIVING ROOM

PAGES 136–37
José Esteves's bespoke table in the form of a large serving tray perfectly showcases the objects displayed. Its four legs are sculpted to resemble the branches of a tree. The blue chairs are Swedish and, behind a Louis XV-style bergère, an eighteenth-century screen is covered in domino paper and gouache prints of works by Boucher.

THE ENTIRE DECOR of this room dates from the end of Louis XV's reign. In his book *Le Port-Louis Revisité* (Port-Louis revisited), the architect Gérard Dieul describes the living room as follows: "The original beams and coffered ceiling are an integral part of the decor, because hanging a ceiling beneath the beams would have reduced the height of the room excessively. The windows and doors are linked by a small, high picture rail, which is interrupted by the fireplace overmantel forming the chimney breast. The paneling in most of the room uses recessed molding, but the large panel over the fireplace features bolection (raised) molding, including a beautiful, sculpted rocaille motif." The fireplace in painted wood, made to look like marble, contrasts with the soft green color palette used on the walls.

The ancient paneling cleverly conceals fitted original cupboards. One of them, designed to look like a cabinet, hides the stairwell leading to the cellar. One narrow cupboard houses a well within the wall facing the street, bringing water directly into the house from the basement. Such a convenience was particularly unusual at that time. This curious feature leads us to believe that this room was originally a dining room. The owner of the house was a wealthy merchant with a large family, who came from a line of seafarers and merchants; by all appearances, he seems to have liked his creature comforts as much as he did high-quality interiors.

KINGSTON
A. V.
PARIS

FACING PAGE
Two eighteenth-century Swedish chairs are arranged around a pedestal table. The statuette on the table—an example of Quimper pottery—depicts a Virgin, unusually without the Christ Child in her arms. This is a "Childbirth Madonna," used as a candle-holder during labor.

BELOW
Pompon, the guardian of the residence. This tiny Havana rabbit has the run of the place.

As one season gives way to another, with the arrival of fall we change the layout of the furniture to make the atmosphere cozier. During this period, we like to bring in the two large, comfortable Louis XV-style armchairs from the small living room in the outbuilding. Following eighteenth-century tradition, we use a period screen, echoing the colors of the living room, to protect ourselves from drafts and add charm to our interior. Several *indienne* fabrics in madder red warm up the ambiance, while for the curtains and cushions we have chosen the "Colonnes" pattern from our linen collection (which adorns the endpapers of this book), inspired by a document from the collector and talented Valérie Hubert. Here it is printed on linen for the curtains and cushions.

The flooring throughout the whole of the ground floor had to be modified. In the 1960s, the original parquet was removed, a concrete screed was poured, and black-and-white tiles were laid on top. This created a rather unsightly clash between the graphic floor pattern and the charm of the woodwork. Technical problems regarding the door thresholds and ensuring the doors would actually close meant that the new floor could not be thicker than ⅘ of an inch (2 cm). The antique salvage dealer we usually go to suggested a compelling solution—a solid wood parquet floor made of original beams that could be fixed directly to the concrete. Planks of three different widths echo the eighteenth-century parquet on the upper floors. The result is magical, as if this floor had always been here, from the beginning.

PORTRAIT

MONIQUE DUVEAU & JOSÉ ESTEVES

CULINARY WIZARDS

When we met Mona and José, our shared tastes in food and interior design quickly created a rapport. Like any devoted couple, Mona and José seem made for each other. They are very close and share a uniquely special gastronomic world, which they have turned into a way of life. Clearly they are the two people who have inspired us most in recent years. In their house—a former church school in a village in Normandy's Le Perche region—they entertain friends with unparalleled generosity. José is a captivating artist, a designer of furniture and light fittings, and a talented photographer in his spare time. Mona works magic with table decorations and floral arrangements, and is an outstanding cook. They both have the rare quality of being constantly curious, marveling at everything as if seeing it through a child's eyes, and they are always happy to share their discoveries in celebratory settings to which Mona alone holds the secret.

Every year, they make their traditional quince cheese. Mona prepares the fruit while José oversees the long and tiring process of cooking the jelly in the saucepan; it needs to be stirred for a long time with a large wooden spoon. They then pour the mixture into small, differently shaped molds. It's a magical sight when they've arranged these little delights on their large kitchen sideboard, and they will later offer them as gifts to their many friends, delicately wrapped, sometimes in scraps of our domino papers that Mona has carefully collected.

A RUSTIC TABLE

FALL IS A SEASON for enjoying food. It's a time when we get ready for winter—jams and bottled fruits and vegetables fill the kitchen and living-room cupboards. The onset of cold weather makes us instinctively want to hunker down by the fireside. On Sunday evenings, after a long walk in the woods, there's nothing nicer than laying a small table next to the fireplace and enjoying the last glimmers of daylight, while roasting the chestnuts we collected on our walk.

Pan-fried girolles with garlic and parsley add a special touch to an impromptu omelet. The Breton sheep's cheese made at La Fromagerie de François's dairy goes perfectly with the quince cheese given to us by our friends Mona and José.

As night falls, we're surprised to find our only illumination is the fire and the candle slowly burning in the top of a blown-glass bottle transformed into a candlestick.

Our dog Lili, curled up snugly on the rug, also enjoys the warmth and tenderness of this precious moment.

ANTIQUING *AT* FLEA MARKETS

VISITING FLEA MARKETS is not about "searching" but about "finding," or rather stumbling across an object that moves us, that speaks to us, and, for some unknown reason, brings us a great deal of joy, even if the object in question is not something essential. Surprisingly, we always agree about what we like.

The more the years go by, the more we favor simple objects—everyday, useful items, such as those commonly called "folk art." It's true that our passion for cooking inclines us first and foremost toward tableware: nutcrackers, bowls, wooden spoons, chopping boards, pitchers, and any other utensil that might encourage our foodie tendencies. However, we might also feel moved when we spot a highly oxidized antique mirror with warm distorting reflections. And even more exciting would be to find a screen covered with faded wallpaper, transporting us to another era.

Our life in Brittany gives new impetus to our discoveries. The many items imported during the time of the East India Company are still very much in evidence here, and it is not uncommon to stumble upon some eighteenth-century Eastern wonders from the estates of traditional Breton families.

THE YELLOW BEDROOM

FROM OUR VERY FIRST VISIT to the house, this room was named the "Yellow Bedroom." As evening came, and light invaded the room, the pale, almost yellow paint on the walls reflected golden hues. A strong yellow seemed the obvious choice, selected from the palette of colors we created that were inspired by the Louis XV and Louis XVI eras. After repainting the walls, we had the idea of hanging wallpaper within each wooden panel. As this was the first bedroom we redecorated, we made the symbolic choice to use the first paper to appear in our collection when *À Paris chez Antoinette Poisson* was created: "Guirlandes de Fleurs." The contrast between the yellow of the woodwork and the indigo blue of the wallpaper is bold, but the result is impressive, to say the least. This rococo-style motif—very much in the spirit of Louis XV—goes perfectly with the made-to-measure, "duchess-style" canopy bed.

Opposite the bed, a beautiful, stately Transition-style chest of drawers, sourced in the town of Mayenne, stands majestically, with a model ship adorning the top. In the drawers, we keep some precious eighteenth-century Provençal quilts that will protect us from the cold when winter arrives.

Resembling an eighteenth-century interior, this room now looks as if it has survived the centuries.

A collection of eighteenth-century Provençal *piqué* quilts are stored in the chest of drawers known as a *commode tombeau*, with an antique model of a three-master ship and some vintage items covered with domino paper displayed on top.

PAGES 156–57
An eighteenth-century linen ikat serves as both headboard and bedspread. On the wall hangs a devotional image of 1782, printed by Perdoux in Orléans, depicting the Virgin and Child.

Provençal quilts, also known as *piqué marseillais*, are slightly different from the quilts called *boutis*, although they are often confused. A Provençal quilt has a layer of fleece between two layers of fabric held together by regular, visible stitching. The fabrics used are mostly printed textiles known as *indiennes*. A *boutis* is made from two pieces of fabric sewn together in such a way as to create a pattern. The shapes created by this pattern are stuffed with cotton, or strands of cotton, to form raised areas. Unlike *piqué*, which is opaque, if a *boutis* is held up against the light its patterns create a play of shadows.

The more intimate proportions of this room, the warm colors, and the reflections of the polished wood lend it a soft warmth. We love hunkering down here in the fall, when the temperatures outside start to tumble. It's a protective cocoon, and the ideal place for a late breakfast on Sunday mornings.

FACING PAGE
Old almanacs in various patterns are kept in a wooden box lined with domino paper.

CREATING *A* CANOPY BED

THIS "DUCHESS-STYLE" bed features a canopy fixed at the head on two columns and suspended from the ceiling at the foot of the bed. This type of drapery was very popular in large residences but could also be found in some more rustic bourgeois houses, using *indienne* or *toile de Jouy* textiles.

We created this canopy in its entirety. It is made from a hemp sheet that we dyed with indigo in the garden, making the most of the summer heat. The advice given by our friend Françoise Beuze was invaluable for carrying out the dyeing process.

The dyed hemp sheet was cut into three strips, corresponding to the three sides of the canopy. The bottom edges were shaped to suggest a gentle wave-like movement, lending the design a Louis XV feel. These strips were lined with fleece to give them thickness and body. A seam was left open at the top to slide in four thin curtain rods, which create the frame. We gave the canopy a quilted look by hand-sewing a running stitch at regular intervals. Copper elbow joints (used in plumbing) brought it all together. The whole canopy was suspended from the ceiling on four small metal chains.

To form a headboard over the large central wall, we draped a length of printed fabric, which we change with the seasons.

A TOUCH *OF* NATURE *IN THE* BEDROOM

TO IMBUE THIS ROOM with elements of the natural world, we added some Louis XIII-style chairs and an antique *verdure* tapestry. Appearing first in the late Middle Ages and highly sought-after, *verdures* enjoyed great success until the eighteenth century.

They combine perfectly with natural materials and pared-down interiors, such as these floor tiles in traditional Breton colors (variegated pink), which we found at our antique salvage supplier's.

Hung above the bed to act as a headboard, the tapestry is very eye-catching and creates a vanishing point in this small room. On either side, the plant-shaped sconces by José Esteves overlap the edges of the tapestry and blend perfectly with the headboard.

FORAGING *FOR* MUSHROOMS

IN FALL, mushroom gathering is a must. Basket in hand, we set out into the woodland undergrowth at the moment when the dew brings out the scents of moss and earth. Keeping our eyes peeled, we pace the paths and slopes, watching for signs of the tiniest fleshy cap beneath the leaves and fallen pine needles. It's like a treasure hunt; gathering mushrooms revives our childlike wonder and stimulates our taste buds. We scour the undergrowth for the bright yellow of girolles, the warm brown of chanterelles, and the velvety texture of porcini mushrooms. Our greatest pleasure is finding the white heads of little field mushrooms amid the green grass of the open meadows.

These morning outings to explore the countryside in the open air are the perfect opportunity to create large bouquets of chestnut-tree branches and russet-colored ferns, to extend our enjoyment of these moments in the natural world once we get home.

Chestnuts mingle with mushrooms in our baskets, alongside a few lichens that we like to arrange on the fireplace like jewels. Their rugged shapes and verdigris color add a touch of primeval nature to the ordered decor of our living room. They are a nod to the baroque artists and artisans for whom nature was an essential source of inspiration.

Lili, the black-eyed border collie pup, enjoys picking mushrooms and playing in the bushes, but her favorite pastime is chasing after sticks!

JACQUES BRÉJOUX

MOULIN DU VERGER

The Moulin du Verger was established in 1539, and is today the very last mill, still in operation, to perpetuate the centuries-old paper-making tradition in the Charente département. Jacques Bréjoux has been making paper on a tributary of the Charente River known as Les Eaux Claires, near Angoulême, for some forty years. Rebuilt in the seventeenth century, the long building is a drying space and, under the vaulting of the mill, the paper pulp is beaten by a large hammer milling machine. To this day, this mill is the only one that makes paper out of old linen and hemp sheets, using the machine that Jacques Bréjoux managed to restore.

For over ten years, Jacques Bréjoux has supplied us with the paper for our prints. He created, especially for us, a paper mold in dimensions that correspond to the "Couronne" format (14⅙ × 18¹⁄₁₀ in./36 × 46 cm), traditionally used for domino papers. Historical and scientific studies have always been a driving force in Jacques Bréjoux's work. But it is perhaps through trial and error that he has succeeded in realizing and fully understanding these theoretical texts. This self-taught master artisan now produces some of the most beautiful handmade papers in the pre-industrial style. We are proud to be playing a part in preserving this skill.

MENU
Roasted Oysters
•
Spit-Roasted
Poularde en Croûte
•
Orange Blossom
Crème Brûlée

Roasted Oysters

SERVES 4
PREPARATION TIME: 5 minutes
COOKING TIME: 5 minutes

INGREDIENTS

12 cupped oysters
3 tbsp (1¾ oz./50 g) butter
Pink peppercorns
Freshly ground black pepper

Preheat the broiler.

Shuck the oysters, pour out the liquor, and separate the oysters from the shells.

Place the oysters in their half-shells in a baking dish. Top each one with about 1 teaspoon (4 g) butter, sprinkle generously with pink peppercorns, and add a few grinds of black pepper.

Place under the broiler for about 5 minutes, until just cooked through.

Serve immediately.

OPINEL

Spit-Roasted Poularde en Croûte

SERVES 6
PREPARATION TIME: 30 minutes
COOKING TIME: 1 hour
RESTING TIME: 15 minutes

EQUIPMENT

Oven with a rotisserie feature
(alternatively, use a grill)

INGREDIENTS

Pastry:
17 tbsp (3½ oz./100 g) salted butter
⅔ cups (7 oz./200 g) all-purpose flour
2 eggs
Water as needed

Filling:
10½ oz. (300 g) poultry liver
3½ oz. (100 g) bread with the crust removed
Scant ½ cup (100 ml) raw cream
2 egg yolks
A few parsley sprigs
A few scallions, thinly sliced
Salt and pepper

To assemble:
1 poularde (2¾ lb./1.2 kg)
15 very thin bacon slices

To prepare the pastry, melt the butter in a saucepan. Add all the flour at once, then remove from the heat and stir vigorously using a spatula. Stir in the eggs and add a little water if necessary, if the dough seems dry. Shape the dough into a ball, cover with plastic wrap, and chill until using.

To prepare the filling, finely chop the poultry liver and place in a food processor with the bread, cream, egg yolks, parsley, and scallions. Season with salt and pepper and process until smooth.

To assemble and roast the poularde, preheat an oven with a rotisserie feature to 350°F (180°C/Gas Mark 4).

Stuff the poularde with the filling and tie it up tightly with twine wrapped around the legs and rump. Cover with the bacon slices.

Roll out the pastry thinly and place the poularde in the center. Wrap the pastry around the bird, covering it completely. Cover with parchment paper.

Place the poularde on the spit, lower the oven temperature to 325°F (160°C/Gas Mark 3), and roast for 1 hour. Remove the parchment paper and continue roasting until the pastry is deeply browned.

Transfer to a serving plate and serve immediately.

Orange Blossom Crême Brûlée

SERVES 4
PREPARATION TIME: 10 minutes
COOKING TIME: 45 minutes
CHILLING TIME: At least 2 hours

EQUIPMENT

4 × 6-in. (15-cm) ramekins

INGREDIENTS

6 egg yolks
½ cup (3½ oz./100 g) sugar
1 tsp orange blossom water
Grated zest of 1 lime
⅔ cup (160 ml) whole milk, well chilled
2 cups (500 ml) heavy cream, minimum 30% fat, well chilled
2 tbsp (25 g) packed brown sugar

Preheat the oven to 195°F (90°C/Gas Mark ¼).

In a large bowl, whisk together the egg yolks and sugar until pale and thick.

Whisk in the orange blossom water and lime zest, followed by the milk and cream. Whisk until well combined and smooth.

Divide the cream mixture between the ramekins, filling them three-quarters full.

Bake for 45 minutes in a bain marie (roasting dish half-filled with hot water), until just set. Let cool to room temperature, then chill for at least 2 hours.

Before serving, sprinkle the brown sugar over the top and caramelize using a kitchen torch or place briefly under the broiler.

B·R

A PARIS CH

ANTOINETTE POISSON.
A PARIS CHEZ
PARIS

Siècle
de
PIERRE le GRAND
1700 à 1800
LOUIS XV

WINTER

THE LIGHT is getting paler, the days are growing ever shorter, and the first frosts make their presence felt. But the winter sun warms our hearts as we sit on a stone bench in the garden, or by the sea on the rocks of nearby Lohic beach.

In Brittany, it never gets very cold, and the mild weather means we can take long walks along the peninsula beside the Small Sea of Gâvres. This haven of peace, once a sardine-fishing port, can be reached by taking the water bus that stops not far from the house.

On the wide expanses of the Small Sea, at low tide we don our boots and, armed with a bucket and rake, we go in search of shellfish. Cockles, clams, and sometimes mussels and wild oysters are ours for the taking, if we're lucky! The harvest is often enough to fill a pan with shellfish, which we then cook in butter, garlic, and parsley.

In late afternoon, it's best to stay inside where it's warm, around a cozy fire in the living room. We snack on gingerbread, along with hot chocolate made according to a 1776 recipe, served on French East India Company tableware.

It's the perfect time to focus on indoor activities. In the kitchen, we tidy the cupboards and dressers and line them with sheets of domino paper. In the small living room, we craft lampshades to light the long winter evenings.

The reverse of the "Retour des Émigrés" (Return of the emigrants) screen that stands in the playroom features two rare late-eighteenth-century wallpapers: one is a pattern of hornbeam leaves in shades of Prussian blue, and the other depicts a crowded bed of China asters. A Greek key and palmetto frieze frames the entire screen.

OPÉRA

THE PLAYROOM

THE PLAYROOM is an intimate space; it is wallpapered with an *indienne* motif called "Mignonette," inspired by an eighteenth-century domino paper from Pierre Bousquet's collection. The wallpaper was hung in the center of the wood paneling, which was painted in a yellow shade we created for Ressource paints. In this room, we have set out some antique toys and childhood souvenirs around the Louis XVI-style bed. At one time, the bed had cane panels, but now it's been upholstered with one of our "Grenades" prints. This was one of our very first test printings on fabric. We printed it using the plates engraved for our domino papers, on rectangles of antique, pre-dyed fabric. The result was very satisfying. However, in order to use it for any kind of interior decoration, other than cushion-making, the printed rectangles had to be sewn together to create larger surfaces. Each headboard panel comprises six pieces, with the pattern carefully aligned.

A few eighteenth-century Provençal quilts made from printed cotton canvas serve as throws and bedspreads; they are layered and show glimpses of bright colors on their underside. On the wall, on hangers, or over the back of a chair, we display waistcoats and a Louis XVI frock coat which we sourced from the Drouot auction house.

On the wall of the playroom, a Louis XVI *habit à la française* men's suit, made of silk drugget, is hung over an embroidered waistcoat from the same period.

The screen—re-covered with wallpaper—is an essential item of furniture in an eighteenth-century interior. It makes it possible, in addition to providing protection from drafts, to partition off areas of a room and provides a certain degree of privacy when the living room is also used as a bedroom or reception room. We acquired this screen, which is decorated with the very first known panoramic wallpaper: a Directoire-period mural called *Le Retour des Émigrés* (*The Return of the Emigrants*) for this room. It tells the story of emigrants returning to France after the French Revolution, still wearing the same clothes they had worn under the *ancien régime*, but now encountering some incredible and marvelous characters dressed in the new fashions. It's one of the rare examples of this panoramic wallpaper, which is only known from its use on folding screens. By an amusing coincidence, we had restored a similar screen in 2008, held in the collection of the Musée Carnavalet in Paris and exhibited in the rooms devoted to the Revolution.

The miniature theater illustrates our taste for opera sets, and the antique toys, such as the card game *Le Nain Jaune* (Yellow Dwarf), and the history-themed puzzles scattered around the room patiently wait for the games to begin.

Also known as *Lindor* during the Revolution, the game *Le Nain Jaune* (Yellow Dwarf) takes its name from the famous dwarf Nicolas Ferry. It is said that Ferry's behavior deteriorated badly as he got older, becoming violent and cruel, and so he was nicknamed the "yellow dwarf," after the villain of the seventeenth-century fairy tale. The game came back into fashion under the Second Empire (the period of the board shown in this photo) and gradually became a classic.

An eighteenth-century embroidered men's waistcoat, the book *Nouveaux Contes de Fées* (*New Fairy Tales*) by the Countess de Ségur, and an elephant from a set of lead circus figurines are displayed on an early nineteenth-century Swedish chair.

NOUVEAUX
NOUVEAUX CONTES DE FÉES
ÉDITIONS TALLANDIER

PORTRAIT

FRAGONARD

MUSEUM OF PROVENÇAL COSTUMES AND JEWELRY

In 1926, Eugène Feuch founded Fragonard, a perfume company named after painter Jean-Honoré Fragonard, whose father was a glove-maker and perfumer in Grasse. Over nine decades, this small artisanal perfume maker went international, with three factories, five museums, and twenty shops. But beyond Fragonard's success in perfumery and cosmetics, we admire their love of heritage and their generosity.

Today, sisters Agnès, Françoise, and Anne Costa manage this magnificent firm and the global cultural program their parents launched to showcase perfumery and Provençal heritage, now synonymous with Fragonard's image. For decades, their mother Hélène Costa collected quality Provençal costumes and jewelry from the end of the eighteenth to the mid-nineteenth centuries, constituting one of the finest collections in France, and the only collection of Provençal costumes open to the public all year.

French eighteenth-century textile printing has close ties with our work. When we visited the Fragonard collection, we had a marvelous, unexpected, and moving surprise. Our friend Clément Trouche, who works for the museum's collections, had dressed a mannequin in a stunning piece the museum had just acquired: a dress made from "*Chiné à la branche*" taffeta, dyed in various colors, with wide, flat pleats in the back, known as "*à la Watteau.*" It once belonged to Madame de Monistrol, wife of Julien Louis de Monistrol (1730–1791), sales controller for the French East India Company in Lorient. This wonderful coincidence was the perfect conclusion to our photo shoots with Ruth Ribeaucourt, an avid collector of Provençal fabrics herself. The tale had come full circle.

CHOK

STYLE TIP

WALLPAPERING *A* CUPBOARD

FROM THE EARLY EIGHTEENTH CENTURY onward, domino paper was used to line alcoves, cupboards, and trunks to create a surprise when they were opened. At that time, using this kind of paper as wall decoration was new, and a response to several practices. It substituted for and improved upon the printed fabrics known as *indiennes*. The latter, banned by Louis XIV in 1686, would only be authorized for import once again in 1759, as a result of pressure from Madame de Pompadour, among others. Domino papers also provided insulation for walls, especially when they were hung in several layers. In cupboards they protected linen from the tannins that leached out of the wood.

The untreated wood interior of our kitchen cupboard needed a contrast with the walls, which had been painted an eggshell white. We printed the domino paper from our collection "Grands Pavots," a wonderfully luxuriant botanical pattern, inspired by a mid-eighteenth-century document. First, the shelves were removed, then the sheets of paper were trimmed on both sides so that they could be aligned with the next sheet. A starch-based paste was applied to the back of each sheet, which was then hung using a roller and brush. The interior was papered sheet by sheet, moving from top to bottom and from left to right. The same technique was used for the insides of the doors. Once everything was dry, the shelves were put back.

This is a simple, fun use for domino paper. It is also an effective method for creating a contrast and transforming a particular spot or furniture—a closet, alcove, library shelves, or other surfaces—into a decorative feature.

café
de Tradition
Madras
Curry
Powder
Serge
Vincent
Toi
CHOKY
CHOKY
CHOKY

Maracuja
BEYER
BEYER
PERFECT SEAL
A PARIS CHEZ

PORTRAIT

NADÈGE GAULTIER & LAURA GONINET

CONFITURE PARISIENNE

Confiture Parisienne was founded in 2015 by Nadège Gaultier and Laura Goninet to perpetuate the work of the capital's artisanal jam makers, who until the early twentieth century were transforming local harvests into pure fruit delights.

In their manufacturing workshop located in the heart of Paris, Nadège and Laura create traditional products with surprising flavors. The excellence of their craft also lies in the choice of fruits, selected from the season's best, and in their use of unrefined sugar. Cooked in small quantities in copper cauldrons using traditional methods, the jams are presented in elegantly decorated, white-lacquered jars to protect them from the light and ensure that they are perfectly preserved.

We met Laura and Nadège to discuss the idea of creating a jam together. Our inspiration came from the cake known as *puits d'amour* (wells of love). Commissioned by Louis XV for Madame de Pompadour, *puits d'amour* contained in its center a kind of jelly made from red fruits and violets. Our fondness for cooking, and for old recipes, plunged us (almost literally) into recreating this jam. For the occasion we designed a very fresh botanical pattern to decorate the packaging.

A TEATIME TABLE

THERE'S NOTHING MORE COMFORTING than a delicious warm afternoon tea after a long walk on the beach dodging the squalls. Our faces still salty from the wintry spray, we enjoy a cup of hot chocolate and a slice of spiced loaf cake. Eastern spices bring the warmth of the sun into the very heart of this cold season. They warm both body and spirit and hint at the promise of travel. At this little makeshift table by the fireside, we're boarding a ship belonging to the French East India Company. A Chinese porcelain cup, nestling delicately in the palm of our hands, transports us to other places and other times. The magic of this historic house captivates us every moment of the day.

An improvised snack is laid out on a pedestal table dressed in a nineteenth-century Indian tablecloth. Hot chocolate is served with gingerbread still warm from the oven and accompanied by Venetian *fritole*, or carnival fritters, in a beautiful eighteenth-century porcelain lidded pot that is decorated with polychrome flowers in reserve on a Capuchin background from the Qianlong period.

CREATING BATHROOM SCONCES

THE PASSAGE LEADING to the ground-floor bedroom has been converted into a bathroom, with a shower on one side and a washstand on the other. Creating this antechamber means that the sleeping area can remain private. In order to retain the rustic feel of the bedroom, we decided to cover all the bathroom surfaces with terracotta tiles, purchased from an antique salvage dealer. The faucets and basin were made in brass and copper by artisans.

In the spirit of recycling and to chime with the coppery reflecting tones, we set out on the hunt for metallic elements to create the sconces. It was in José Esteves' incredible workshop in Le Perche that we found a tangle of metallic oak leaves once used in bridal crowns. By forming them into harmonious rosette shapes using metal wires, we created discreet, elegant, and botanically themed lightbulb covers that complement the tones in this small bathroom.

PATCHOULI

ANTOINETTE POISSON

HANDCRAFTING LAMPSHADES

WINTER IS THE IDEAL TIME for minor decorating and craft projects. Conical lampshades have always been part of the *Antoinette Poisson* world, inspired by antique originals made from enameled metal. Starting with sheets of papier-mâché, we came up with the idea of making our own lampshades and covering them with domino paper. This reproduced the lightness, opacity, and resistance of metal.

The papier-mâché is cut into a half-moon, in the shape of a lampshade. It is assembled and covered with domino paper. Some hand-painted mesh adds the finishing touch. The lampshades can be hung from a brass gripper, or fixed over a lightbulb using a copper lampshade clip.

These shades can be used on table lamps or floor lamps such as José Esteves' slender creations. A mixture of patterns can also be fitted over the bulbs of a chandelier to create a dramatic effect.

A PARIS CHEZ — ANTOINETTE

ANTOINETTE
CHEZ — ANTOINETTE POISSON. — N°16
N°16

GATHERING SHELLFISH

SHORE FISHING is practiced all year round in the Small Sea of Gâvres, except in summer. Setting off from the house, wearing our boots, we reach these open beaches and begin a veritable treasure hunt. The Small Sea of Gâvres is a three-mile-long (5 km) saltwater marsh forming a fourteen-acre (560 ha) basin that fills and empties completely with each tide. It is famous for its fauna and great diversity of flora, including, in particular, the salt-marsh plants, which cover a large expanse of the basin.

At high tide, when the tidal range is over 295 feet (90 m), it is advisable to arrive one to two hours before low tide. Armed with a collecting bucket, we scratch away at the sand with a scraper and rake, or sometimes with our hands.

Cockles live in colonies on muddy or sandy shores, and are abundant in this environment. They can be spotted in the small rivulets that form as the tide goes out, or where birds are delving into the sand. If we're lucky, we'll also find clams, mussels, and wild oysters, some of which can be impressively large.

We return home content, having gotten our fill of fresh air—all the more so if our fishing expedition has provided us with a decent meal!

MENU
Roasted Scallops
Pigs' Trotters & Langoustines
Puits d'Amour
Teatime

Roasted Scallops

SERVES 6
PREPARATION TIME: 10 minutes
COOKING TIME: 3 to 5 minutes

INGREDIENTS

6 to 12 scallops in their shells
2 tbsp (1 oz./30 g) lightly salted butter
1 scant tsp (2 g) Kari Gosse spice mix
or *piment d'Espelette*

Ask your fishmonger to open and clean the scallops, leaving the coral attached if you wish.

Preheat the broiler.

Select 6 nicely cupped shells and place one or two scallops in each, with the coral attached if you desire.

Place 1 teaspoon (5 g) of butter on each shell and a pinch of Kari Gosse spice mix or *piment d'Espelette*.

Place under the broiler for 3 to 5 minutes, until the scallops are just cooked through (they should be opaque throughout).

Serve immediately.

Pigs' Trotters & Langoustines

SERVES 4
PREPARATION TIME: 30 minutes
COOKING TIME: 30 minutes

INGREDIENTS

2 shallots
½ tbsp (15 g) butter
2 pigs' trotters cooked in court bouillon by your butcher
1 handful kosher salt
24 langoustines, or around 60 shrimp (prawns)
1 sheet puff pastry
1 generous tbsp (20 ml) sunflower oil

Peel the shallots and chop them finely. Melt the butter over low heat in a large skillet, then add the shallots and cook until softened and browned.

Meanwhile, debone and remove all the cartilage from the pigs' trotters. Roughly chop the meat.

Add the chopped meat to a skillet with the shallots. Cook until the gelatin has dissolved and the meat is golden and caramelized on the edges.

Fill a large saucepan with water, add the kosher salt, and bring to a boil. Add the langoustines (or shrimp/prawns) and cook for 3 to 4 minutes, until they change color, then plunge into a bowl of ice water to stop the cooking. Peel and reserve for assembly.

Preheat the oven to 340°F (170°C/Gas Mark 3). Using a large round cookie cutter, cut out four puff-pastry disks; scallop the edges if you wish. Place on a baking sheet lined with parchment paper and pierce all over using a fork. Bake for 15 to 20 minutes, until golden.

Set a puff-pastry disk on each plate and place a mound of the pigs' trotter mixture in the center of each (use a stainless-steel ring mold if you'd like clean edges).

Decorate with the shellfish, brushed with a little oil to make them glossy.

Puits d'Amour

SERVES 4
PREPARATION TIME: 50 minutes
COOKING TIME: 20 minutes
CHILLING TIME: 20 minutes

EQUIPMENT

2-in. (5-cm) and 1¼-in. (3-cm)
round cookie cutters

INGREDIENTS

Puff pastry wells:
10½ oz. (300 g) puff pastry

Pastry cream:
2 cups (500 ml) whole milk
1 vanilla bean, split lengthwise
2 egg yolks
½ cup (3½ oz./100 g) sugar
2 tbsp (20 g) all-purpose flour
2 tbsp (20 g) cornstarch

To assemble:
Generous ½ cup (7 oz./200 g) red berry jam
5 drops violet extract
¾ lb. (350 g) pastry cream (see above)
Granulated sugar for sprinkling

Roll the puff pastry to a thickness of about ¼ inch (5 mm). Using the 2-inch (5-cm) cutter, cut out sixteen disks. Using the 1¼-inch (3-cm) cutter, cut circles out of the centers of eight of the disks. Reserve the cut-out circles for decoration if you wish.

Very lightly brush with water the undersides of the puff-pastry disks that have had the centers cut out. Lay them on the uncut disks, taking care to line up the edges. Place on a baking sheet lined with parchment paper. (If you're using the cut-out circles for decoration, place on the baking sheet and score with an attractive pattern.) Chill for 1 hour before baking.

Preheat the oven to 350°F (180°C/Gas Mark 4). Bake the pastry wells until puffed and golden (about 20 minutes).

Meanwhile, prepare the pastry cream. Pour the milk into a large saucepan, add the vanilla bean, and bring to a simmer.

Whisk together the egg yolks and sugar in a large bowl until pale and thick. Whisk in the flour and cornstarch. Whisking gently, slowly pour in one-quarter of the hot vanilla-infused milk. Return to the saucepan, whisking continuously. Let the mixture simmer for 1 minute, whisking vigorously to prevent it from sticking to the bottom of the pan.

Pour the pastry cream into a shallow dish and immediately press plastic wrap over the surface. Let cool to room temperature, then transfer to the refrigerator to chill.

To assemble, stir the violet extract into the jam. Fill the wells with pastry cream and spoon jam over the top. Sprinkle sugar over the jam and place under the broiler for 1 minute to caramelize, watching closely to ensure the sugar does not burn. Top with the decorated cut-out pastry circles if using. Serve chilled.

Spiced Loaf Cake
by Christiane Martin

SERVES 6
PREPARATION TIME: 15 minutes
COOKING TIME: 1 hour

EQUIPMENT
10-in. (25-cm) loaf pan

INGREDIENTS
1 cup (250 ml) honey
¾ cup (200 ml) water
1⅔ cups (7 oz./200 g) all-purpose flour
Scant ⅓ cup (1 oz./30 g) rye flour
1 pinch salt
2 level tsp baking soda
⅓ cup (2½ oz./75 g) packed brown sugar
½ tsp ground spices of your choice
(star anise, cinnamon,
quatre-épices spice mix, etc.)

Preheat the oven to 350°F (180°C/Gas Mark 4) and line the loaf pan with parchment paper. Warm the honey and water in a saucepan over low heat until the honey dissolves.

In a large bowl, combine the flours, salt, baking soda, brown sugar, and spices. Gradually whisk in the honey mixture. Whisk vigorously until well blended and frothy. Pour into the prepared loaf pan.

Bake for 15 minutes at 350°F (180°C/Gas Mark 4), then lower the heat to 325°F (160°C/Gas Mark 3) and continue to bake for an additional 45 minutes. Do not open the oven door before the end of the baking time. Let cool for 10 minutes in the pan, then turn out onto a rack and let cool completely.

Venetian-Style Rice Fritters

SERVES 6
PREPARATION TIME: 15 minutes
COOKING TIME: 45 minutes
RESTING TIME: 1 hour

INGREDIENTS
4 cups (1 liter) whole milk
1 vanilla bean, split lengthwise
⅔ cup (4¼ oz./120 g) short-grain rice
⅓ cup (2½ oz./70 g) sugar
2 tsp cornstarch
3 eggs, beaten
1 apple (preferably Reinette),
peeled and finely diced
Scant ¼ cup (1 oz./30 g) Zante currants
Oil for frying
Confectioners' sugar

Pour the milk into a large saucepan, add the vanilla bean, and bring to a simmer. Add the rice and cook for 45 minutes, stirring often to prevent a film from forming. When the rice is completely tender, remove it from the heat. Take out the vanilla bean and stir in the sugar, cornstarch, eggs, apple, and currants. Let cool to room temperature.

Dip your hands into water and shape the rice into small balls the size of walnuts.

In a saucepan, heat the oil for frying (it should be deep enough to fully immerse the rice balls). Test the temperature by adding one rice ball. The oil is ready when bubbles form around it. Cook the rice balls in the oil for about 5 minutes, until golden all over. Drain on paper towel and dust with confectioners' sugar. Serve warm.

A PARIS CHEZ
TE POISSON. — N°24
A PAR

ANTOINETTE POISSON.
N° 7
CHEZ
ANTOINETTE POISSON.

ADDRESSES

À PARIS CHEZ ANTOINETTE POISSON
12 Rue Saint-Sabin
75011 Paris

Le Bon Marché Rive Gauche
Maison, second floor
24 Rue de Sèvres
75007 Paris

Port-Liberté
5 Rue de la Poste
56290 Port-Louis

For the complete list of international retail outlets, see www.antoinettepoisson.com/en/points-de-vente/

ANTIQUITÉS DÉBARRAS DE L'OUEST
59 Avenue de la République
56700 Hennebont

An absolute Aladdin's cave full of vintage objects associated with Brittany and the sea, this antiques store helped us acquire furniture and tableware from the French East India Company.

AXS DESIGN
12 Rue Saint-Sabin
75011 Paris

Created in 2017 by Ariel Novak and Sydney Sabatier, AXS Design came about from the meeting of two vintage enthusiasts who are experts in collecting and showcasing objects. Their store contains a wide range of domestic items, dating from the 1900s to the 1990s.

BRUNO LE YAOUANC, ANTIQUAIRE
Marché Paul Bert
alley 5, stands 208 & 210
93–110 Rue des Rosiers
93400 Saint-Ouen

We visit Bruno's stand for tastefully reupholstered seating and beautifully patinated Dutch furniture.

CARNOT ANTIQUITÉS
6 Rue Auguste Nayel
56100 Lorient

Furniture and tableware imported by the French East India Company.

CHARMES DE LA MAISON
—interiors & antiques store
29 Rue de la Libération
56410 Étel

Christine Geffroy's store sells secondhand furniture and unusual objects.

CONFITURE PARISIENNE
17 Avenue Daumesnil
75012 Paris

Nadège and Laura have been using high-quality produce to create extraordinary jams in their laboratory-cum-store since 2015.

DIPTYQUE
34 Boulevard Saint-Germain
75005 Paris

Creator of perfumes and scented candles, Diptyque was originally founded by three artists who decided to sell their own fabric and wallpaper designs, showcased in a store selling items they had brought back from overseas.

FRANÇOIS MASSON
2 Place au Bois
56290 Port-Louis

François Masson is an expert restorer and maker of baroque wind instruments.

LA FROMAGERIE DE FRANÇOIS
5 Grande Rue
56290 Port-Louis

François's dairy sells a wide range of farmhouse cheeses from Brittany and other regions, as well as raw milk and high-quality dairy products.

GALERIE STÉPHANE OLIVIER
3 Rue de l'Université
75007 Paris

This gallery in Saint-Germain-des-Prés stocks antique furniture often inspired by the natural world, and Scandinavian pieces from the 1950s to the 1970s.

GOLFE AGENCEMENT
80 Rue Alain Gerbault
56000 Vannes

We met the team at Golfe Agencement, a carpentry company capable of handling a wide variety of projects, when we took on the artistic direction of the Château de Versailles store in collaboration with Romain Chauveau of Supercraft.

GUCCI
Gucci Garden
Piazza della Signora 10
50122 Florence
Italy

The leather goods and fashion brand has opened a museum devoted to the company's history from 1921 to the present day in the Palazzo della Mercanzia.

JOHN DERIAN COMPANY
6 East Second Street
New York, NY 10003
USA

Since 1989, John Derian and his team have used *découpages* (cut-outs) to create glass-topped objects in his New York studio. His Manhattan boutiques stock his work alongside that of other designers, decorative objects for the home, and antiques.

JOSÉ ESTEVES
@joseesteveslights

José Esteves is an artist and craftsman who designs and makes furniture and light fittings inspired by the natural world. He produces unique, bespoke pieces.

LADURÉE
21 Rue Bonaparte
75006 Paris

Located at the historic 21 Rue Bonaparte address in a store that once belonged to the great interior designer Madeleine Castaing, this company is legendary.

LASCOMBES MATÉRIAUX
1 Rue Henri Duverdin
78200 Soindres

Heritage craftworkers for thirty years, Lascombes Matériaux specialize in traditional materials such as wooden beams, fireplaces, parquet floors, tiles, and flagstones. They helped us to refurbish the wooden flooring on the ground floor of Maison Lescop.

MOULIN DU VERGER
—handmade paper mill
Chemin du Moulin du Verger
16400 Puymoyen

The Moulin du Verger is one of the oldest paper mills in the Charente département and boasts a long tradition of papermaking. Jacques Bréjoux is one of the few people still using old sheets in the process of manufacturing paper.

MUSÉE DE LA COMPAGNIE DES INDES [MUSEUM OF THE FRENCH EAST INDIA COMPANY]
Citadelle de Port-Louis
Avenue du Fort de l'Aigle
56290 Port-Louis

The Museum of the French East India Company presents an extensive panoramic history of the companies, their exploits, and the goods they brought back from the East.

MUSÉE PROVENÇAL DU COSTUME ET DU BIJOU [THE MUSEUM OF PROVENÇAL COSTUMES AND JEWELRY]
2 Rue Jean Ossola
06130 Grasse

The museum is one of the few establishments devoted exclusively to the traditional clothing and jewelry of historic Provence.

LES PARCS DE NAVIHAN
—oysters & shellfish
5 Rue Navihan
56550 Belz

Les Parcs de Navihan sells farmed and wild oysters and shellfish in season, stocked in cold-water tanks.

PHARMACIE DE PORT-LOUIS
—Kari Gosse
8 Grande Rue
56290 Port-Louis

Like many pharmacies in Morbihan, this store sells the famous blend of spices created by Kari Gosse in the nineteenth century.

POISSONNERIE DESCHAMPS
17 Grande Rue
56290 Port-Louis

The freshest local fish and shellfish—customers visit every day to stock up.

RESSOURCE
87 Boulevard Beaumarchais
75003 Paris

A French brand that has pioneered the manufacture of high-end decorative paints, Ressource is the choice of professionals and all those who love sophisticated interior design.

LA SOUFFLERIE
7 Rue de l'Odéon
75006 Paris

La Soufflerie is a non-profit association of glassblowers set up by Sébastien and Valentina Nobile. Today, La Soufflerie produces a complete range of glassware alongside plaster, terra-cotta, and wood items, and hand-poured candles.

SUPERCRAFT STUDIO
38 Rue de Trévise
75009 Paris

Romain Chauveau uses space, light, and high-quality materials to enhance what already exists, while showing respect for both the building and the materials themselves—which he managed to do brilliantly during the renovation of Maison Lescop.

TÉLÉSIÈGE
6 Rue des Lilas
56670 Riantec

An excellent upholsterer making curtains and seat coverings.

TOPTOP CÉRAMIQUE
36 Boulevard Joliot Curie
44200 Nantes

Ceramicists Marie Wiart and Lucas le Roy create unique, colorful pieces in their Nantes workshop.

INDEX *OF* RECIPES

APPETIZERS

MAIN COURSES

DESSERTS

TEATIME SNACKS

ACKNOWLEDGMENTS

RUTH RIBEAUCOURT
THE PHOTOGRAPHER

As we have often said, "we understand each other." We couldn't have dreamed of a better photographer to illustrate our project. From the first photos she took, it was clear that this collaboration was meant to be. Ruth's photography reveals the soul of our house without betraying all of its secrets.

A collector of eighteenth-century Provençal textiles, Ruth visited Maison Lescop for several photographic sessions, bringing some of her collection with her, which admirably complemented our mise-en-scène. With our shared passion for eighteenth-century crafts, the partnership was bound to succeed.

An Irishwoman who has lived in Provence since 2010, Ruth launched a jewelry collection inspired by vintage textiles, which quickly brought her international recognition. At the same time, and thanks to her growing network of contacts, Ruth began to take photographs and write articles about designers for lots of magazines. By creating and guest-editing a special issue of *What Women Create*, focusing on the idea of slowing down and healing through creativity, Ruth found her purpose—to give creatives a platform and a voice. *FAIRE* magazine was born in spring 2021 and enjoyed immediate success.

DEDICATION

WE DEDICATE THIS BOOK to our entire team, without whom the crazy adventure of *À Paris chez Antoinette Poisson* would never have become what it is today. Thanks to Sophie Begon-Fage, Axelle de Fabry, Christel Derrien, Pauline De Smet, Charlis Giraud, Catherine Montagne, Magali Perruchini, Catherine Prevost, Isabelle Saget, and the interns who have crossed our path.

We are very grateful for the people we have around us.

To our parents, for having encouraged us to enter the world of the arts from a very young age.

Thank you to the whole team at Flammarion for having faith in us, for having encouraged our project from the very start, and for the ease of our discussions. Thank you to Jean-Loup Champion for initiating this project, and for introducing us to this wonderful publishing house.

Thank you to Romain Chauveau and his interior design studio, Supercraft, for their help in restoring Maison Lescop.

Thank you to Françoise and Patrick Morgan for opening their home to us.

Thank you to Clara Luciani, François Masson, Françoise Beuze, John Derian, Monique Duveau and José Esteves, Jacques Bréjoux, Anne, Agnès, and Françoise Costa, and Nadège Gaultier and Laura Goninet for their portraits. Many more people took part in this project and helped us enormously. We are particularly grateful to Caroline du Pin de Saint-André, Morgane Sézalory, Alessandro Michele, Lyn Harris and Christophe Michel, Alix Depondt Reynis, Myriam Badault, Valérie Hubert, Fabienne Nomine and Pascal Bisson, Clément Trouche, Pierre Bousquet, Pierre Sauvage, Cécile Coquelet, Jean-Michel Le Claire, Don Carney, and John Ross.

To our closest friends who have always supported us on our journeys: Annaé Annenkoff, Cécile Gombaud, Jean-Louis Roblin, Ariel Novak, Sydney Sabatier, Anne-Marie Geffroy, Nathalie Mémeteau, François Roy, François Ardouvin, Christine Laureau, Emilie Tolsau, Karine Larue, Marie Thurnauer, Frédéric Smektala, Marie-Odile Roy, Philippe Pistole and Jean-François, Blandine and Bruno de Mareuil, Jeanne, William, and Caroline Cabannes, Yves di Domenico, and Martin Kiefer.

To all those, both near and far, who have fed our imagination, lent a helping hand, supported us, and who will recognize themselves in our work. And finally, to our growing number of clients around the world, for having faith in us.